Lord, I Can Resist Anything But Temptation

Also by Harold Busséll–

Unholy Devotion: Why Cults Lure Christians

Lord, I Can Resist Anything But Temptation

Harold L. Busséll

Zondervan Publishing House
Grand Rapids, Michigan

Lord, I Can Resist Anything But Temptation

This is a Pyranee Book
Published by the Zondervan Publishing House
1415 Lake Drive, S.E., Grand Rapids, Michigan 49506

Library of Congress Cataloging in Publication Data

Busséll, Harold L.
Lord, I can resist anything but temptation.

Bibliography: p.
1. Temptation. 2. Christian life—1960– . I. Title.
BT725.B87 1985 241′.3 84-29149
ISBN 0-310-37271-2

Edited by Kathy Heetderks
Designed by Ann Cherryman

Printed in the United States of America

85 86 87 88 89 90 / 10 9 8 7 6 5 4 3 2 1

*To my parents, LaVern and Verna-Valeria Busséll,
and my in-laws, Edwin and Edna Markwalder,
who by their lives have modeled over the years
faithfulness, conviction, and compassion.*

Contents

PREFACE 9

1. Breaking Sin Myths 13
2. The Temptation to Virtue 21
3. The Temptation to Authenticate Self 33
4. The Temptation to Test God 47
5. The Temptation to Expediency 61
6. The Temptation to Reject Forgiveness 75
7. Seeing Yourself Through the Eyes of God 93
8. Why Do I Keep Falling—Just When I Overcame? 113
9. The Gift of Self-Control 133
10. Building a Fortress Against Temptation 151
11. Living in the World—But Not of It 167
12. Experience Your Future in the Present 187

NOTES 195
BIBLIOGRAPHY 199

Preface

I experienced my first bus ride as a first grader. I was invited to join a group of students from my grammar school to visit a museum some thirty miles away. Once on the bus, I immediately ran to the back to join the sixth graders. I idolized them. They were mature and smart: they sat at the back of the bus. But I was rejected: too little, too young.

After an eternity of five years, I arrived. I sat in the back of the bus with the other sixth graders, making faces at passing cars and enjoying the thrills of back-seat bouncing as the bus hit potholes. Much of the pleasure, however, was in the position. From the back of the bus I could condescend to the younger ones: "Sorry, you're just too little, first graders."

But then I found myself starting to envy the ninth graders, who seemed macho and independent, so free from sudden voice changes, from clumsy limbs, from fear of girls.

As a ninth grader . . . yes, there were the twelfth graders telling me I was too young to ride in the back of the bus. So growing up, partly, was one bus ride after another, always with the hopes of "arriving" at the back of the bus.

For us in the pastorate, our eyes also often focus on those "successful" types who seem to be free from family struggles, temptations, personality quirks, and insecurities. Regardless of which calling we have in life, there are always those at the back of the bus who seem to have arrived. Now that I am in my forties, I still find myself walking to the back of some bus or other, only to hear—or, let me confess, imagining to hear—the condescending response from some successful pastor: "Sorry, you are just too little. Maybe someday you will arrive and be able to enjoy the back of the bus."

Many Christians live their lives like that, trying to find some back of the bus or other, looking for some new method, insight, or secret to rid them forever of their insecurities, internal battles, and struggles with temptation. Unfortunately, at the back of every bus they find the sixth graders giving cheap answers, or easy affirmation.

I have written this book for Christians who struggle with various temptations and have been disillusioned by the simplistic answers and putdowns given at the back of the bus. My hopes are that you will understand that, as it was with our Lord, so it is with us: life is a constant challenge with new struggles, tests, and temptations. If we are going to resist the Evil One, it is important to understand how he operates even in the back of the bus.

We fight a unique battle. Our concerns are not the same as those of the Roman Christians who worshiped in catacombs and sought to escape the attacks of those who worshiped gods carved in wood and stone. Our call is to remain sane and Christian in an age that tries to carve its idols in our minds.

Acknowledgments

Thanks to—

Mr. Louis A. Larson, who has encouraged me for ten years to write.

Mr. Paul Borgman for his encouragement, insights, and help on the manuscript of this book.

Mrs. Kathy Heetderks for editing the manuscript.

Those who wish to succeed must ask the right preliminary questions.

—*Aristotle*

If any person seeks for greatness, let him or her forget greatness and ask for truth, and he or she will find both.

—*Horace Mann*

1.

Breaking Sin Myths

Within each of us rages a civil war. People who have appeared to be responsible may suddenly act irresponsibly, committing acts of sin. Why? Because each of us struggles with temptation.

Temptation can place us in a seemingly hopeless and frustrating situation from which there is no apparent escape. Coupled with the awareness of complete helplessness is the feeling that we should not be there in the first place.

Throughout time, everyone has struggled with temptation. The struggle for some is like a fight for air by a drowning person. Others claim to be beyond the struggles of temptation—but these, without knowing it, have succumbed to the temptation of spiritual pride.

Christ himself, who never stepped out of the will of God, was not free from temptation. Late in his life Jesus was taunted by a crowd echoing Satan's tempting offer: "If you are the Son of God, prove thyself."

Luke is particularly sensitive to the temptations that Christ had to face. In some of his very last words Christ reminds the disciples of their share in his ministry's difficulties: "Ye are they which have continued with me in my temptations" (Luke 22:28 KJV).

Many people experience unnecessary frustrations and guilt when facing temptation. They believe particular temptations are peculiar to *them*, or they assume that there are easy solutions which somehow have eluded them. They keep expecting, wrongly, that temptations will subside with time and maturity. Many books, articles, and seminars promise simple steps for facing temptation, only to set us up for unnecessary failure. (Scripture does not record Jesus or Paul holding seminars on five easy steps to overcoming temptation.)

We may be tempted when we least expect it. Adam and Eve passed that special tree every day. Yet, as James Stalker writes, "One of the chief powers of temptation is the power of surprise. It comes when you are not looking for it; it comes from the person and the quarter you least suspect. . . . No bell rings in the sky to give warning that the hour of destiny has come."[1]

Paul warned Timothy and the believers in Corinth "to flee temptation, to run from it" (for example, 2 Timothy 2:22). But what is it? How does it operate? To understand that, we must identify and challenge the various myths Christians believe about temptation. These myths are often as seductive as temptation itself.

For example:

"Mature Christians Seem to Be Immune to Temptation"

At a ministers' luncheon in Boston, an animated discussion arose concerning an issue of *Leadership* magazine (Fall 1982) which had focused on the topic of temptation. In an article entitled "The War Within: An Anatomy of Lust," a presumably well-known evangelical leader, writing anonymously, came clean on the besmirched history of his sexual struggles.

There was a variety of reactions to the article. Many were couched in tones of dismay: "I am shocked." Why the shock? Either these pastors are naïve, or they have not been reading their Bibles carefully enough. The Bible is realistic in its treatment of sin and redemption. There is little place for the words "I am shocked" in biblical thinking. We all have various lusts, sexual or otherwise, in the menagerie of our thoughts.

I *did* think that the article was in poor taste, though I felt compassion for the enslavement and despair this pastor had experienced. The article described in vivid detail all the antics and events that transpire in a live porno-peep show. To curious minds, the article could have added fuel to the fires of lust; in this sense the exposé was itself pornographic.

But should we be shocked? Never. All our deeds and thoughts will be exposed someday. God knows our thoughts, our feelings, our fantasies toward good, and our fantasies toward evil. Shock implies self-deception—and vulnerability to the ploys of Satan. To be shocked is to admit we believe the myth "Mature Christians are immune to temptation."

Another myth:

"Sin Just Isn't Fun"

At the age of twelve I attended my first Christian summer camp. The route to camp took us through the center of San Francisco. The driver of the bus took us on a tour of the city's skid row. Several drunks were digging through garbage cans for a little food or a few lost coins for some more liquor. Our bus driver's wife stood up and gave us a long lecture on the evils of sin. She kept repeating over and over, "Children, sin just isn't fun."

Ironically, I cannot remember her other words, but I can remember passing a building with a billboard of Marilyn Monroe advertising a certain product. I was only twelve . . . but I remember that her dress was black and that a question was slowly forming in my mind: "If sin isn't fun, why are so many people sinning?"

We believe a myth if we think that sin is no fun. That

is why the lure of temptation is often so painful. It is true that the results are ugly, that relationships are broken, and that the self is finally destroyed. But it is a myth to believe that the act of sin itself is not fun. There is an immediate rush of pleasure when we experience our own power. To believe the myth that sin is never fun precludes the possibility of dealing with sin and its temptations.

"I Fell Into Sin"

"Oh, I just fell into sin." Never believe it. Temptation may hit us by surprise. However, sin is not an accident. It is not a camouflaged hole that entraps us. Most of the time, in fact, we plot our own falls.

Perhaps the greatest barrier to resisting the temptation leading to sin is our conscious and subconscious resistance to the truth about ourselves. Jay Adams points out, "Just as sinful Adam first thought of lying his way out of difficulty, it is perfectly natural for the natural man to develop patterns of falsehood. We only add to the complexity and difficulty of relationships when we deceive ourselves."[2] Self-deception leads to *apparent* "falls" into this sin or that.

Lack of self-awareness leads to a lack of other-awareness. We dare not confront others because of what we fear to face in ourselves. Jay Adams suggests one aspect of the problem: "Communication at the most essential level of all, in the direct confrontation of one person with another, has never been as superficially unauthentic and unsatisfying. In the midst of plenty, it seems there exists a famine of genuine communication."[3] As we refuse to deal honestly with ourselves, we likewise resist God's recreative work in our lives and hence the possibility of restored relationships.

"Temptation Will Leave With Maturity"

When I mature in my faith, goes a naïve hope, temptation will leave and I will be trouble free. Many Christians are destroyed emotionally because of this myth.

Jack spent several years in counseling because he suffered from low self-esteem. He had been a pastor for twenty years when suddenly he felt his world collapsing. While his ministry and life appeared well run and successful, his inner self was falling apart. What was the problem? Mainly, guilt and frustration because he felt something must be wrong with his faith. Operating in his mind was a myth that nearly ruined him and his family. He simply assumed that with time and maturity temptation would leave.

A close study of Scripture will reveal that this is not the case. As Christian wayfarers, in fact, we discover greater challenges the farther we travel. John White writes,

> Temptation will always change its masks—business for some, sensuality for others, riches for the middle-aged, power for others, resentment for those who hurt, unhealthy fantasies for those who feel trapped. The evil one can bring the changes with greater skill than any advertising agency. He knows the Achilles' heel of every microbe. You will be tempted continuously. You will be tempted ferociously at times of crisis. Jesus himself was tempted "in all points as we are" (that is, to commit adultery, to steal, to lie, to kill and on and on) yet without sin.[4]

Spiritual maturity is, in this context, the mastery of elementary temptation in preparation for advanced testings.

"This Once Won't Hurt"

"This once won't hurt" is a myth that drives us to live for the moment. The rationalization which accompanies this myth is that one act does not affect history.

However, choices made today influence the choices of tomorrow. So it is that character develops—or fails to.

Few couples go to the altar saying, "Let's get a divorce in five years." An alcoholic seldom says with his or her first overindulgence, "Well, I think I will become an alcoholic." Our past choices shape the present, and the present builds into the future.

At first an act of sin requires an effort and is soon followed with regret. But the voice of conscience and the breath of God's Spirit, if ignored, are diminished if the evil deed is multiplied. Deterioration is a process. St. Paul's language on the subject suggests the path of this process: thinking *becomes* futile; one *becomes* a fool; one begins to replace the glorious mirrors of God's nature with decaying images of dying nature, and so on.

Paul addresses the results of following this myth in his letter to the church in Rome:

> For although they knew God, they neither glorified him as God nor gave thanks to him, but their thinking became futile and their foolish hearts were darkened. Although they claimed to be wise, they became fools and exchanged the glory of the immortal God for images made to look like mortal man and birds and animals and reptiles. . . .
>
> Furthermore, since they did not think it worthwhile to retain the knowledge of God, he gave them over to a depraved mind, to do what ought not to be done. They have become filled with every kind of wickedness, evil, greed and depravity. They are full of envy, murder, strife, deceit and malice. They are gossips, slanderers, God-haters, insolent, arrogant and boastful; they invent ways of doing evil; they disobey their parents; they are senseless, faithless, heartless, ruthless. Although they know God's righteous decree that those who do such things deserve death, they not only continue to do these very things but also approve of those who practice them (1:21–23, 28–32).

Choices become habits. Habits either prepare us to flee temptation's darkness for the light, or they pave the way for increasing darkness.

The fact is that every temptation to evil will probably come wrapped in a myth of virtue. Bishop Fulton J. Sheen writes,

> The caresses by which the lustful seduce each other are disguised as love; curiosity passes itself off as a desire for knowledge; laziness calls itself a love of solitude and rest; wastefulness presents itself as generosity; enviousness as a legitimate wish to excel; cruelty, as a love for justice; and pride, as loftiness of spirit. The first downward step comes when we deceive ourselves, accepting a lying label which makes an evil thing seem good to us.[5]

It is in our ears that evil lies, and it is from our hearts that it must be plucked out.

—*Bertrand Russell*

Nothing is more seductive for man than his freedom of conscience. But nothing is a greater cause of suffering.

—*Dostoevsky*

2.

The Temptation to Virtue

Vice and Virtue

C. S. Lewis once said, "The worst temptation is the temptation to virtue, not evil: a virtue that goes unchecked is much more dangerous than a blatant evil. A blatant evil makes you feel guilty, but a virtue makes you feel proud."[1] Liberation from destructive living or new spiritual insights are opportunities for Satan to tempt us to condescend to others who have not experienced the same new lease on life. The temptation will be to build a new elite fellowship that spends its time complimenting each other while holding in contempt the unredeemed or unlearned. Elitism blinds people both to the needs of others and to their own arrogance. Elitism is the root source of most racism, arrogance, family feuds, church divisions, and hostility. At its core, elitism finds its identity in opposition to others.

As a child I was fascinated by the stories of visiting missionaries who had spent time in prisons or concentration camps during World War II. They seldom referred to their sufferings. Great leaders throughout church history—those we call "saints"—seldom speak of their own spirituality. Many assume that these saints went around with folded hands. A close examination of their lives, however, reveals that they often hid their virtues. Their lives were not marked by desires to impress others.

Have you read stories about people who have become self-made, wealthy tycoons? One of these stories usually begins by relating how the hero started in abject poverty and gained wealth, much to his own surprise. What is fascinating about these people is that they seem to appreciate their poverty only when they have gained wealth. They have confused "having something" with "being somebody."

Love Self at Others' Expense

None of us is free from the Tempter's seduction to feel better about oneself at someone else's expense. The moment we overcome besetting sins, understand new truths, or discover new abilities, the danger is to yield to Satan's call to be arrogant. What becomes important is not the new truth, but the temptation to prove ourselves as being right or superior. Satan tempts the righteous, the gifted, and the caring to substitute arrogance for character.

God gives us gifts, and then we are tempted to take those gifts and define ourselves "better" in opposition to the "worse"—the "have nots."

Susan, a caring person, loved to help people in need. Life for Susan had always been marked by compassion, concern, and care. She enjoyed bringing food and flowers to people in need. However, over a period of years, that virtue slowly became a vice. Susan's identity ultimately became dependent on the approval given for her sacrificial gifts of love. On one occasion someone failed to say "Thank you," and immediately a volcano of resentment, hurt, and anger erupted. What was the problem? Susan's virtue had become an enslaving vice.

The Bible records this temptation clearly in several places. The realism of the Bible is to be admired. It describes the human condition, not as people may like to have it described, but as it is. Think of the disciples who rejected and were even ready to kill the Samaritans:

> As the time approached for him to be taken up to heaven, Jesus resolutely set out for Jerusalem. And he sent messengers on ahead, who went into a Samaritan village to get things ready for him; but the people there did not welcome him, because he was heading for Jerusalem. When the disciples James and John saw this, they asked, "Lord, do you want us to call fire down from heaven to destroy them?" But Jesus turned and rebuked them, and they went to another village (Luke 9:51–55).

Like the rest of us, the disciples were blind to the forces of temptation hidden within their virtues.

An interesting chain of events in the life of King David is recorded in the Old Testament. Twice David faced a challenge to destroy Saul, a chief enemy (see 1 Samuel 24 and 26). David's friends encouraged him to do it. His compassion, however, ignited a unique response. David cut off a piece of Saul's robe to be used later as a sign of David's desire for mercy. He rested the case in God: "Vengeance is the Lord's."

> So David and Abishai went to the army by night, and there was Saul, lying asleep inside the camp with his spear stuck in the ground near his head. Abner and the soldiers were lying around him.
>
> Abishai said to David, "Today God has delivered your enemy into your hands. Now let me pin him to the ground with one thrust of my spear; I won't strike him twice."
>
> But David said to Abishai, "Don't destroy him! Who can lay a hand on the LORD's anointed and be guiltless? As surely as the LORD lives," he said, "the LORD himself will strike him; either his time will come and he will die, or he will go into battle and perish. But the LORD forbid that I should lay a hand on the LORD's anointed. Now get the spear and water jug that are near his head, and let's go" (1 Samuel 26: 7–11).

This virtue later became for David a vice that brought misery into his home.

Amnon was a demanding child controlled by emotions. He wanted to have sexual relations with Tamar, his half-sister. Amnon's friend, Jonadab, encouraged him to act sick in order to entrap Tamar and take advantage of her. Tamar, desiring dignity, tried to address the exploitation by placing ashes on her head. Where was David? He avoided the conflict. David's virtue, to not take vengeance, became a vice. Why? David had a habit of not exercising discipline where his family was concerned. The Bible says that *he was furious*; but he did nothing about it.

David failed to protect his daughter's dignity. However, Absalom—Tamar's brother—remained angry with Amnon and two years later planned his murder. The painful results of avoidance led to the issue. Jonadab, the person who gave Amnon the idea, then became David's spiritual counselor and encourager (2 Samuel 13).

David had suspicions about the situation, but gave in to the temptation to avoid confrontation. David asked Absalom why he wanted to take Amnon along, but failed to confront the basic issues at stake. Satan used David's virtue as a weapon. As a fearless leader he had refused to avenge himself on others, but he allowed this great virtue to become the factor that destroyed his family.

Qualities of character can be used by the Tempter as destructive forces. Compassion can turn into an emotion of control. We can be tempted to use love as an excuse for compromise. A deep sense of justice can become a weapon for cruelty.

Paul Tournier sees this issue as basic to many conflicts. In *The Violence Within,* he writes,

> Look at the photographs of other convoys of troops setting off for other wars that have quickly ended in disaster. The scene is the same: Is it just the universal love of adventure, or the considered resolve to fulfill a

patriotic duty? Is there not also a certain pleasure at being authorized, even urged, to commit what up to then has been forbidden? I do not mean expressly to kill, the thought of which is hardly conscious, but to be violent.[2]

Understanding Pride

Several years ago a young college student sang Mozart's *Allelujah* at a pastor's conference in Boston. Her performance evidenced practice, thought, and prayer. After the service I complimented the student. A pastor standing nearby commented, "Remember, youth frequently forgets that pride goeth before a fall." But is it pride to want to do well for God? Is not the goal of all believers to hear Christ's words, "Well done" (Matthew 25:14–30)? I took issue with the pastor's spiritual putdown. I contended that the performance was not an example of pride. The sense of accomplishment we experience when we do an excellent job for Jesus Christ is not pride. Perhaps the pastor's comment offered a clearer example of pride.

Pride is an attitude that causes people to pass from saying "I have done well" to "I am better than others." Pride is dependent on relationships. It needs others, in an unhealthy way; it is dependent on others for exaltation of the self. Like the elder brother in the parable of the Prodigal Son, pride finds its meaning only by opposition to a presumed "inferior." Like a fungus, it depends on other life to exist.

Pride prevents healthy relationships with God or others. It makes beautiful and gifted people ugly. It lies at the core of most gossip. The person who gossips builds up self by tearing down others. Pride can take a church blessed by God and make its members into arrogant prudes. Pride takes virtues, blessings, gifts, and insights and turns them into indexes used to feed its sense of superiority. Pride always has an *er* added: prettier, better, richer, smarter.

We all face the temptation to have pride. It is

expressed in a variety of ways. The Tempter enslaves us to it when we least expect it to be a part of our lives. Its potholes can jar loose the very framework of our relationships and identity. The Devil tempts us when we have experienced something good like overcoming temptation to some other vice.

C. S. Lewis once wrote,

> The Devil is perfectly content to see you become chaste and brave and self-controlled, provided all the time he is setting up in you the dictatorship of pride.[3]

Yes, chastity, self-control, compassion, and love can become the cancers that destroy the possibility of appreciation for others' accomplishments. Was not this the problem of the pastor—a gifted singer himself—when he said, "Remember, youth frequently forget that pride goeth before a fall"? The young woman was not indulging pride by being pleased with doing well for Christ. She faces pride only if she identifies herself in opposition to another singer. Pride has been the spiritual infirmity that has sabotaged and destroyed relationships the most throughout history.

Understanding Jealousy

Anyone who has lost a large amount of weight knows about temptation. Whether the loss comes through diets, exercise, or medication, the temptation to sin will be there. What sin? Contempt. For each pound we lose, we gain another pound of contempt for people whose waistlines do not fit the guidelines of the "Tab generation."

This appeal to one-upmanship is the basis for much advertising. The temptation is first to break the tenth commandment by coveting. On the surface it is an appeal to virtue, but at its root it seeks to keep us in the throes of a new vice. The barrage of thirty-second commercials tempts us with promises of good looks, thin bodies, irresistible power over others, and perhaps, upward mobility. However, what may appear on the surface to be self-help or upward mobility could accomplish the very opposite, producing self-hatred. Those instant ads often spot and spoil our vision of reality, resulting in much frustration and self-contempt.

One of the difficulties of middle age is that our dissatisfaction in life often arises, not with the evils we have suffered, but with the goods we cannot attain. The aging process forces us to see that many of the goods and goals we had hoped for will never be realized. Hopes were colored over the years by ads that led to coveting. This can ignite in any person, regardless of age, a fire of jealousy. Jealousy is basically self-hatred. It's the reverse form of pride. Jealousy does not elevate us in opposition to others, but to ourselves.

Jealousy Is Inward

Jealousy is pride turned inward. It is pulling the pin on the hand-grenade of pride and then holding on to destroy ourselves. Jealousy causes us to hate ourselves: not as beautiful as Brooke Shields, not as handsome as Tom Selleck. Pastors hate themselves because they are not as successful as another pastor. Laypeople hate themselves because they are not as spiritual as another; "only a housewife"; middle-aged; merely an average provider. Many voices tempt us to hate ourselves for the good we cannot attain: that trip to Bermuda, accomplished children, a successful or prestigious vocation, a more spiritual home, affluence, or beauty.

Doesn't this temptation lie at the core of many difficulties we face in life? Pastors tear others down because they secretly hate themselves for not being as disciplined, successful, or gregarious. Believers discount the validity of others' spiritual experiences or walk with God because they secretly hate themselves for not being as dedicated or concerned. People gossip about others' failures. Aren't these just different ways of saying, "Thank God, I am not like one of them"?

Looking for Pure Motives

The Tempter can also tempt us into believing that we do all things out of only pure motives. Don't buy that proposition. If you do, you will eventually lose your footing and fall off the cliff of self-deception. I can offer an example in something I struggle with. We who have been gifted by God with ability to speak publicly, to teach or preach, must not be naïve: we never do anything totally out of pure motives. We can have a tremendous sense of power when hundreds of people are listening and cannot answer back. We can become obsessed with trying to purify all motives and be left with pietistic pride or be blinded by our need to control and impress people.

These are all examples of pride. Pride is the undue estimation and inordinate esteem of our own excellence in comparison with others or God. External gifts and even inward marks of character can become the weapons of Satan. Pride elevates our relative character into an absolute. Pride is the carbon copy calling itself the original. Satan feeds the caged animal of pride on virtues entrusted to us by the Creator.

Pride and jealousy alienate us by giving us a false feeling of independence. When we are unable to achieve superiority in real life, we can be tempted by Satan to live in a fantasy world of superiority. A college student preparing for a final examination may perceive that she cannot realize her fantasy and thus develops a sickness. If well, the student would be forced to prove the intelligence of which she boasted. Failure to receive an "A" means she must give up the pretense of superiority.

This problem was basic to the church in the first century. It is precisely this ailment that Paul addresses in a letter to the Corinthians.

> My brothers, some from Chloe's household have informed me that there are quarrels among you. What I mean is this: One of you says, "I follow Paul"; another, "I follow Apollos"; another, "I follow Cephas"; still another, "I follow Christ."
>
> Is Christ divided? Was Paul crucified for you? Were you baptized into the name of Paul? (1 Corinthians 1:11–13).

What was the Corinthians' problem? Did not Peter, Christ, Paul, and Apollos preach the same message? Of course they did! The Corinthians simply redefined themselves in opposition to each other. Are our temptations any different?

Have you ever used these words or heard them from others?

> "Oh, I am charismatic!" "Oh, we are not charismatic."
>
> "I am high church." "We have spontaneity and give the Spirit freedom to move in our church services."
>
> "We have broadened our thinking and have joined a nondenominational denomination." "Not us, we don't stoop to any labels."
>
> "We are of Christ." "I am Baptist." "I am Methodist."
>
> "You mean you have never been to a leadership institute?"

Time has not healed the Achilles heel of the Corinthians.

When Right Goes Wrong

We will never be completely rid of the temptation of one-upmanship. It was this sin that challenged the disciples in the garden just before the Crucifixion. Jesus had taken them with him to pray, and later, finding them sleeping, he asked, "Could you men not keep watch with me for one hour? Watch and pray so that you will not fall into temptation" (Matthew 26:40–41). What temptation? Before the evening passed, they would be tempted to use their ideas of justice as weapons of destruction.

Soon after Jesus issued his admonition, the silence was shattered by shouting voices and glowing lanterns. A large crowd of slaves, servants, soldiers, and religious leaders confronted the little group. Why so many? There were only a dozen men in the garden. Did Judas tell them something about the disciples? The disciples had weapons of violence under their robes; one of them succumbed to temptation and cut off the ear of a slave. Jesus, hearing the cry, reached out, touched, and healed the man (Luke 22:49–51).

We can become fascinated by this miracle and overlook an important issue: The disciples were armed with weapons of violence and were tempted to use them. Under their robes of discipleship were the weapons of vice. We tend to envision these disciples as hiking through the quiet fields of Galilee while serving and following Christ. But in this situation they carried weapons into a peaceful garden. Their sense of justice had become a vice.

The Garden of Gethsemane was not as tranquil as it might be described in Sunday school lessons. It's easy to romanticize that night. But it was a time and a place where Christ was deeply troubled about his coming ordeal and the temptations facing the disciples. Jesus had warned them and encouraged them to pray that "they would not fall into temptation." His concerns proved to be well-founded. The crowd came armed, the implication being that they suspected they would encounter resistance. The disciples even asked Jesus, "Lord, should we strike with our swords?" (Luke 22:49). It must have been a night of great confusion—people shouting for blood while crying for justice.

Jesus cried, "No more of this!" The Gospel According to Matthew adds his words, "All who draw the sword will die by the sword" (26:52). The cause of truth will not be advanced by the vice of violence. That is almost a truism. But neither will truth be advanced when virtue becomes a vice.

God calls us to place checks and balances on our virtues lest we succumb to temptation through the back door.

Udo Middleman sums it up well:

> When we understand how much God gives us and when we understand that our call is to be faithful to that to which he has called us, then we are free to start looking at each other. Then we can begin to practice the care of each other and even to rejoice with others when they have more than we do. We get more of a feel for the totality of man and for the fallenness of history and for all the suffering that is in the world. Then we will not be looking at ourselves and feeling dreadfully sorry.
>
> Then we will see how much God gives us, how really good God is to us individually. We will see that other people are depressed and other people are tired and other people have problems, and we can come together to God and share, not by comparing ourselves with others but by rejoicing in the things God has given to each of us. We can begin to rejoice with thanksgiving because life as God granted it to us is indeed good. And of course, the Christian has a unique hope.[4]

Jesus Christ knew the disciples better than they knew themselves when he said, "Pray so that you will not fall into temptation" (Matthew 26:41).

A man entirely unconcerned with self is dead; a man exclusively concerned with self is a beast.

—*Abraham Heschel*

However brilliant an action, it should not be esteemed great unless the result of a great motive.

—*Maxims*

3.

The Temptation to Authenticate Self

A New Look at Christ

Most Christians try to respond to Scripture's call to be conformed to the image of Jesus Christ. Many fail, however, to look beyond their own images of Christ to the Christ of Scripture. Jesus is often assumed to be a passive, unfeeling stoic, living beyond ordinary pains and hurts. A closer look reveals a far different Christ. He did not avoid conflict and temptation; he faced them head-on.

Jesus established relationships with people who were broken: cheats, hypocrites, social outcasts. The Lord's statements were often cutting—offensive to his natural family as well as his religious family. Our Lord's emotions ran the gamut: anxiety could rupture capillaries, mingling blood with perspiration. He experienced despair and alienation. From his birth—fleeing to Egypt to avoid state-imposed infanticide—to the state-imposed Crucifixion, conflict was the norm. Conflict was always present: conflict between the inner will and the will of God, conflict between his will and the disciples'.

Like us, Jesus was vulnerable in ordinary and human ways. He walked, lived, and ate in the same world we awaken to every day. In contrast with various first-century forms of religious escapism, John declared, "The Word became *flesh* and made his dwelling among us" (John 1:14). Jesus encountered every struggle and temptation known to humankind. The author of the letter to Hebrew Christians tells us,

> Because he himself suffered when he was tempted, he is able to help those who are being tempted (Hebrews 2:18).
>
> For we do not have a high priest who is unable to sympathize with our weaknesses, but we have one who has been tempted in every way, just as we are—yet was without sin (4:15).

It is hard for us to think that Jesus was tempted by lust, greed, power, fornication, or murder, but he was, while remaining sinless. If that is true, then temptation itself is not sin; we can be tempted and still be guiltless.

Life has its storms, interruptions, irritations, ill-treatment, disease, and temptation. Jesus came into our stormy world. Before the dust settles on your latest tempest, remember that our Lord faced wind-whipped storms. There are times when we struggle with temptation but easily forget that conflict, confrontation, and stress were common experiences that our Lord faced throughout his life on earth.

The writer of Hebrews vigorously declares, "Although he was a son, he learned obedience from what he suffered" (Hebrews 5:8). The temptations, conflicts, and confrontations all played an important part in Christ's identification with us. John Knox stated,

> That the son of God was thus tempted gives instruction to us that temptations, although they be ever so grievous and fearful, do not separate us from God's favor and mercy, but rather declare the great graces of God to appertain to us.[1]

Temptation Is Always With Us

Our biblical reflections need to include more than the Sermon on the Mount, parables, and healings of our Lord. Woven throughout these events is a continuous record of conflicts, struggles, attacks, and disappointments. Jesus did not live in a secluded ashram, sealed off behind cloister walls, spouting romantic and sentimental concepts of spirituality. The Word became utterly flesh (John 1:14).

Throughout history, humankind has been trying to reverse this truth, trying to make the flesh spirit, a matter of mere words. To do so breaks down our defenses against temptation. If we fail to examine Jesus' battles with temptation, we will lack the understanding and power to transcend the attacks of Satan.

Matthew's account points up the ironic way that temptation often confronts us. In the first temptation, Jesus was enticed to turn stones into bread.

> And a voice from heaven said, "This is my Son, whom I love; with him I am well pleased."
>
> Then Jesus was led by the Spirit into the desert to be tempted by the devil. After fasting forty days and forty nights, he was hungry. The tempter came to him and said, "If you are the Son of God, tell these stones to become bread."
>
> Jesus answered, "It is written: 'Man does not live on bread alone, but on every word that comes from the mouth of God' " (Matthew 3:17–4:4).

Jesus faced these temptations just after an overwhelming confirmation by God. God declared pleasure with Jesus' development as a human being. Jesus was past his youth and his training as a carpenter when God said, "This is my Son, whom I love; with him I am well pleased." Did spiritual bliss immediately follow? No. Jesus was led into the desert of human experience and temptation. Confirmation, then confrontation. His pattern is ours.

We must not think that in one campaign Jesus drove away the Tempter forever. The Gospel writers give us a record of continual confrontation between the Holy Spirit and Satan, with Jesus the focus of this struggle. For example, the Tempter spoke against Jesus at Caesarea Philippi when Peter tried to dissuade him from taking the way of the Cross (Mark 8:31-33).

I have met many people who are distressed because they have not reached a point of spiritual maturity beyond temptation. They feel that they somehow have not proved themselves truly "spiritual." They hope to soar, like Jonathan Livingston Seagull, beyond all limits of reality—beyond conflict, struggle, and pain. But Jesus never got beyond the possibility of temptation, and neither will we. We all face similar conflicts. There are times when we seem to be in a wilderness where God is strangely silent. Our landscapes appear barren, our deserts unfruitful. We grow frantic to "prove" ourselves. We hunger for it.

Living by the Prove-It Principle

The urge to prove ourselves lies at the heart of temptation. It tugged at Jesus in the wilderness encounter with the Devil. The Prove-It Principle in action: "If you are the Son of God . . ." Jesus faced this same temptation during the grievous torments on the cross.

> In the same way the chief priests, the teachers of the law and the elders mocked him. "He saved others," they said, "but he can't save himself! He's the King of Israel! Let him come down now from the cross, and we will believe in him. He trusts in God. Let God rescue him now if he wants him, for he said, 'I am the Son of God.' " In the same way the robbers who were crucified with him also heaped insults on him (Matthew 27:41–44).

Prove it! The gods of our age shout the same call. On a thousand talk shows, dozens of seminars, and in simple "how-to" booklets, we are called to prove our worth. The appeal to ego strikes at the heart of each person's identity. For example, in a variety of ways we are made to believe that we are what we produce. This leads to a preoccupation with products, visible results, tangible goods, and progress. It is difficult to abandon this preoccupation, since we do not recognize it as a temptation. Henri Nouwen writes,

> We make ourselves believe that we are called to be productive, successful, and effective individuals whose words and actions show that working for the Kingdom is at least as dignified an occupation as working for General Electric, Mobil, Digital, or the U.S. Government.[2]

But has not God already affirmed our worth in creation and redemption?

Meeting Needs in Wrong Ways

The cry to Prove It grows out of our essential ego needs. These needs were all given and affirmed by God in Creation: hunger, sex, love, possessions, acceptance, recognition, work, self-esteem, relationships. For us to be fulfilled in this life, these needs must be met. However, when we fail to follow God's design for fulfilling them, we are headed for trouble. The results of following Satan's bidding are self-destructive; we are hindered in our relationships with others and with God.

One basic need, for example, is recognition. Recognition is fundamental to emotional and spiritual health. Some people spend their lives weaving others into their neurotic webs to gain recognition in destructive ways.

Bill's experiences in Vietnam had scarred him deeply. Flashbacks of bombings, painful deaths, and dismembered bodies plagued him continually. After much prayer, counseling, and encouragement from his pastor, doctor, and family, he began to recover. In the process of his recovery the church prayed. Support groups formed and called him weekly. Under this care Bill subtly built all relationships around this problem. Even when struggles were not there, Bill would fabricate them to receive attention from others.

Eventually Bill's greatest battleground became, not the problems he had in Vietnam, but the support he received afterward. He had legitimate needs for concern, care, and counsel—as we all do. In time, however, Bill required a need in order to have friends. He eventually began to test love from others by how they responded to one of his fabricated crises. He had fallen victim to the temptation to meet legitimate needs in unhealthy ways.

This problem is basic to all temptations. This device of Satan can threaten us in every aspect of our existence. Any need can be met in a sinful and manipulative way. Each is a subtle theme and variation on the same tune: Prove It.

Isn't the call of much advertising an appeal to prove ourselves by meeting legitimate needs in illegitimate ways? We are lured to prove ourselves through sex appeal, material possessions, problem possessions (like Bill's), and a host of other forms of falsely verifying our worth and acceptance.

Satan tempts us to opt for bread alone. He tempts us to serve things, use people, and forget God. God promised these things: "But seek his kingdom, and these things will be given to you as well" (Luke 12:31). Satan promises them to us too, as he did in the temptation of Jesus. But Satan seeks to make us feel that we are being deprived of our daily bread. The gods of this world tempt us to "worship and serve the creature more than the Creator" (Romans 1:25 KJV). Satan makes fulfilling our ordinary needs the motivation for our lives rather than our using them as gifts from God the Creator.

Calvin explains how this happens:

> Christ did not lose his glory as he was exposed to temptations, nor when he put on himself our flesh. Thus the sense of the words is: when you see yourself abandoned by God, necessity forces you to look out for yourself. So provide yourself with food, as God fails to provide it for you. Even if Christ exerts his divine power which turns the stones to bread, the sole object of Satan's game is to move Christ away from God to follow the dictates of infidelity.[3]

Temptation calls us to make needs into gods. But we are not to live in frantic states of anxiety about our food, drink, and clothing. Our identity is to be found in Creation and Grace. We find it by meeting our needs in appropriate, legitimate ways.

The Problem of Authority

Yielding to the temptation to Prove It shortcuts God's way of affirming us, of meeting our needs. We are tempted to sidestep God's grace by taking authority into our own hands. A second truth we learn from Jesus' first temptation is that it is an assault on authority. Satan did not say, "Pray to the father that he would turn the stones into bread." Rather he said, "Command these stones." Isn't your power legitimate? Isn't your hunger legitimate? Isn't bread legitimate for meeting hunger needs? Isn't God, then, depriving you of legitimate wants? So whispers Satan in our ears.

Notice that Satan was trying to bribe Jesus to build a ministry around getting rather than giving. The temptation could not be avoided: the desert was littered with little round pieces of limestone rocks that looked like small loaves of bread. The resemblance would have been obvious to Jesus. The temptation was to build ministry and use power selfishly for personal authenticity. The Roman authorities distributed free bread to promote Caesar's kingdom. Perhaps Jesus could do the same and win the acceptance of the needy masses.

Dostoevsky sees the question by Satan as a clever offer involving more than full and satisfied stomachs.

> Choosing bread, thou wouldst have satisfied the universal and everlasting craving of humanity to find someone to worship . . . Does thou know that the ages will pass, and humanity will proclaim by the lips of their sages that there is no crime, and therefore no sin; there is only hunger?
>
> Feed men, and then ask of them virtue. That is what they'll write on the banner, which they will raise against thee, and with which they will destroy thy temple. But seest thou these stones in this parched and barren wilderness? Turn them into bread and mankind will run after them like a flock of sheep, grateful and obedient, though forever trembling lest thou withdraw thy hand and deny them thy bread.[4]

Jesus refused to fall for the trick. He would not be lured into justifying his claim to authority. But the temptation that confronted him also confronts us. Consider this example:

While living in California, I had a neighbor who campaigned against pornography. I concurred with her zeal. But to inform others of what was being sold in local supermarkets, she would buy a copy of every pornographic magazine she could find. Her family-room floor was stacked with the publications. The very first thing she would tell visitors—with a smirk—was how awful this filth was. In her fight against Satan's values she had become pornographic. She could hardly wait to get others to join her in her campaign. The bait she offered was a good "show-and-tell" experience.

At the heart of this woman's dilemma was the temptation to prove herself. She felt a need to justify her crusade, even to the point where virtue became a vice. She responded to Satan's challenge to God's authority by yielding to the temptation to sidestep dependency on God and authenticate herself by a cause.

What this means can be demonstrated from Jesus' experience. Notice that in responding to Satan's command to turn stones into bread, Jesus did not enter into oratorical debate on the legitimacy of bread. He did not discuss the evils of utilitarianism in a philosophical argument.

Perceiving Satan's art and malicious subtlety, Jesus gave a single, forthright, unambiguous response. He used Scripture. There in the wilderness he used words that God had spoken to his chosen people in their wilderness many centuries earlier: "He humbled you, causing you to hunger and then feeding you with manna, which neither you nor your fathers had known, to teach you that man does not live on bread alone but on every word that comes from the mouth of the LORD" (Deuteronomy 8:3).

Only God's Word, declared in the power of the Spirit, is able to block Satan. When we try to fight Satan with human weapons, we may unwittingly allow him to enter through the back door. In each of us lies the possibility of becoming contaminated in our crusade against evil—which is what happened to my neighbor in California.

Two Kinds of Legalism

The temptation to self-authentication manifests itself in still other ways. Specifically I have in mind legalism. We have already seen that Jesus did not become a legalist and ban the use of bread. He was not "against bread." In responding to Satan, Jesus did not create an index of bread denial cards to be signed by his followers as signs of orthodoxy. He did not become legalistic. He negated neither bread nor the need for it. Nor did he do the opposite and throw out all the rules governing its use. The latter, however, is what trapped my neighbor; indulgence in violation of the authority of the conscience proved to be her undoing.

It is all too easy for a decision to indulge in something

or to abstain from it to be used as a sign of spiritual authenticity. At the core, either can be a way of proving ourselves. Even when we make such a decision out of a sincere desire to become better people, it is possible for the Tempter to feed our human tendencies toward rebellion and independence from God.

The apostle Paul addresses this issue in a letter to the church in Rome:

> Accept him whose faith is weak, without passing judgment on disputable matters. One man's faith allows him to eat everything, but another man, whose faith is weak, eats only vegetables. The man who eats everything must not look down on him who does not, and the man who does not eat everything must not condemn the man who does, for God has accepted him. Who are you to judge someone else's servant? To his own master he stands or falls. And he will stand, for the Lord is able to make him stand (Romans 14:1–4).

Paul describes a situation in which two believers hold opposite views on some basic matters of Christian liberty. Paul sees the danger on either side of saying that we are doing certain things or abstaining from them in order to "please the Lord." Actually it is a means of enhancing ourselves in the eyes of others.

> He who regards one day as special, does so to the Lord. He who eats meat, eats to the Lord, for he gives thanks to God; and he who abstains, does so to the Lord and gives thanks to God (Romans 14:6).

The most important feature of Romans 14 is that Paul decides nothing. He refuses to put his stamp of approval on either side. Paul is dealing in a different setting with the same issue that faced Jesus during the wilderness temptation. And that issue is the Devil's attempt to lure us into self-authentication by what we do or don't indulge in. Whether the substance of the temptation involves restrictions on food or the custom of observing certain days (see Romans 14) doesn't matter. Paul is indifferent. He sees a greater issue at the core of Satan's attack: dependency on God.

> For none of us lives to himself alone and none of us dies to himself alone. If we live, we live to the Lord; and if we die, we die to the Lord. So, whether we live or die, we belong to the Lord. For this very reason, Christ died and returned to life so that he might be the Lord of both the dead and the living (Romans 14:7–9).

"To the Lord" is the touchstone of all of life. Just in case these believers forget that dependency is the basic and central issue Paul says,

> You, then, why do you judge your brother? Or why do you look down on your brother? For we will all stand before God's judgment seat (Romans 14:10).

We need to realize the importance of self-judgment. Both the strong and the weak—those who partake and those who abstain—can use their decisions as signs of self-authenticity. Paul reminds his readers that each person will have to stand before God alone. The whole fabric of the Bible is woven around this issue of dependency on God. All that we do must be done in light of the fact that we either live or die unto the Lord. Abstinence or indulgence is not the primary issue. Dependence is.

Jesus, who refused to respond to the Tempter's call to make bread, not only made bread for the hungry crowds later on, but also instituted it as a sign of this dependency. As his followers gathered around the table at the Lord's Supper, they ate bread and acknowledged needs as their common denominator. Whether we be rich or poor, black or white or brown, educated or uneducated, male or female, we must all eat, or die.

In the act of eating we reveal our backgrounds. Colonel Sanders and Emily Post would not eat fried chicken in the same manner. In eating they revealed their heritage, their culture, their values. However, the common denominator and commonality is that they had need.

As we hold that piece of bread in our hands during Communion, it is not for utilitarian means, but in acknowledgment of a common denominator—the need to rely on God for forgiveness. When I hold that bread, I declare my dependency. I acknowledge that I am dependent on tangible things outside myself. Adam and Eve used food as a sign of rebellion; Christ, the second Adam, instituted bread as a sign of relationship.

We are not called to Prove It, but to acknowledge our need for God's sovereign grace and to respond in faith and dependency.

Those who make religion their god will not have God for their religion.

—*Thomas Erskine*

Spiritual warfare is as brutal as human warfare.

—*Rimbaud*

4.

The Temptation to Test God

> Then the devil took him to the holy city and had him stand on the highest point of the temple. "If you are the Son of God," he said, "throw yourself down. For it is written:
>
> " 'He will command his angels concerning you, and they will lift you up in their hands, so that you will not strike your foot against a stone.' "
>
> Jesus answered him, "It is also written: 'Do not put the Lord your God to the test' " (Matthew 4:5–7).

When his call to live by a Prove-Yourself Principle failed to ignite a response, Satan tempted Jesus to live by the Prove-God Principle. Basically the temptation was to test God by catering to a "claim-it-by-faith" mentality. Satan's idea was for Jesus to create a problem, forcing God to intervene supernaturally, and claim a spectacular victory. In other words, Satan called Jesus to be a religious huckster, God's conman.

Claim It by Faith

Religious frauds are nothing new; they have been with us since Eden. At the core of much religious fraud and deception is this temptation to prove God. The crowd-convincing claim-it-by-faith miracle could have provided Jesus with a great marketing base for evangelism.

Religious conartists are not a new phenomenon. They have sought to dupe God's people throughout the last two millennia—and before. The early church was familiar with several examples, among these noted by William Barclay: "Theudas had led the people out and had promised with a word to split the waters of the Jordan in two [see Acts 5:36]. A famous Egyptian pretender (Acts 21:38) had promised that with a word he would lay flat the walls of Jerusalem. Simon Magus, so it is said, had promised to fly through the air and had perished in the attempt."[1]

These pretenders offered a sensational spirituality that they could never deliver. True spirituality and sensationalism are mutually exclusive.

People have always been tempted by and willing to follow religious conmen. This was precisely Dostoevsky's main point in the Grand Inquisitor passage of *The Brothers Karamazov.*

> And yet if there has ever been on earth a real stupendous miracle, it took place on that day, on the day of the three temptations. The statement of those three questions was itself the miracle. If it were possible to imagine simply for the sake of argument that those three questions of the dread spirit had perished utterly from the books, and that we had to restore them and to invent them anew, and to do so had gathered together all the wise men of the earth—rulers, chief priests, learned men, philosophers, poets—and had set them the task to invent three questions, such as would not only fit the occasion, but express in three words, three human phrases, the whole future history of the world and of humanity . . . dost Thou believe that all the wisdom of the earth united could have invented anything in depth and force equal to the three questions which were actually put to Thee then by the wise and mighty spirit in the wilderness?[2]

One need not go far in the present day to see these same promises of the spectacular. People who refuse to believe in the true God but need something to believe in opt for the greatest show on earth. Many in our own generation, both educated and uneducated, lack the means to discern lies from truth. They become unwitting dupes of dazzling shows of fads and religions. People have sacrificed their minds, lives, pocketbooks, and families because they succumb to the temptation to follow the spectacular.

This temptation to Prove God is sometimes obvious, sometimes subtle. A faith community in the southern United States tests God by handling poisonous snakes. A woman in Miami supposedly had a vision of a great tidal wave engulfing and destroying the whole city; followers sold homes, left good jobs, abandoned families, and moved to Tennessee. The wave still hasn't come. In Flint, Michigan, a group of followers waits for the resurrection of their leader Bernard Gill, who died several years ago. Gill claimed to be one of the two witnesses described in Revelation 11. In New York City the police entered an apartment and found members of a cult praying over the decomposed body of a friend who had died of cancer two months earlier. These are flagrant examples, but they are also countless.

More subtle cases have as strong appeal: "We believe that God will be faithful in getting you all to give, meeting the dollar goal." "We're trusting God to be faithful" (to meet *our* desires, *our* need to be vindicated). This thinking views God as the Faithful Fund Raiser—with a huge edifice or program or numbers count proving that "God is with us."

Similar stories are recorded every week in various sectors of our society. In the religious sector, however, there are those who teach that one need not believe at all. During recent decades many seminaries and churches in America and Europe have set aside eternal verities of the Christian faith in attempts to be relevant.

The vacuum left by this teaching is not a match for the Sierra Club, Sunday golf, Miami Beach, or the Aspen ski slopes. The worshipers have left in droves to attend the temples of palm trees, jagged peaks, and mirrored lakes. We can only wonder who is more stupid—the snake handlers or the prophets of naturalistic faith?

Religious environments—liberal or conservative, Protestant or Catholic—will never protect us from the temptation to be relevant. Choosing the temple as the arena of his temptation of Jesus was a masterstroke of Satan. It underscores the subtlety of his methods.

Jerusalem was the place where God's Word was manifest in the past. It was in this City of Peace that sacrifices were offered, the temple was built, and David and Solomon reigned. This holy city stood as a monument to the past and a promise for the future.

> The Temple was built on the top of Mount Zion. The top of the mountain was leveled out into a plateau, and on that plateau the whole area of the Temple buildings stood. There was one corner at which Solomon's porch and the Royal porch met, and at that corner there was a sheer drop of four hundred and fifty feet into the valley of the Kedron below.[3]

This hub of religious activity was the setting for Satan's second temptation of Jesus. At the temple the priests would blow the trumpets in their hands to call the people to worship. After the call to worship, people would be streaming into the temple in Jerusalem. What an ideal place and time for Jesus to display his power—to prove God for all to see! Come up with a problem where no problem exists, and then claim God's rescue to verify this great act of faith. The crowd would be susceptible, for only the most religious would be at the temple. Of course the people would follow. If God really approves of you, prove it. Make a display; the people will be yours.

This was prime time in an era before TV. The unique

opportunity to prove this new claim-it-by-faith spirituality might come only once. Absurd? Not at all. Jesus was being tempted to use a popular faith method that is practiced widely in some charismatic circles today. It is called the Positive Confession Principle. This practice encourages believers to take selected verses from the Scriptures as their own record or promises from God. These are often coupled with admonishments to remember that "God must honor his Word."

This was the same temptation that faced the Larry Parker family. In his book, *We Let Our Son Die* (Harvest House, 1980), Larry records the tragic story of the devastation his family experienced when their diabetic eleven-year-old son died.

Why did the boy die? Because the family "by faith" withheld his insulin. They were encouraged by friends and pastor to take this step of faith. Where did this tragedy happen? In an evangelical community. Larry Parker records this agonizing struggle for an adequate faith in hopes of preventing similar needless tragedies.

Satan was calling Jesus to create a crisis. He chose the temple and the divine Word for this temptation to test God. He used the Positive Confession Principle.

> He will command his angels concerning you, and they will lift you up in their hands, so that you will not strike your foot against a stone (Matthew 4:6).

In quoting Psalm 91:11, the Evil One omits the important second half of the verse: "to guard you in all your ways." The conditions of protection are clearly described by the Psalmist: provided one follows God's appointed ways, and not any other. When Satan quotes Scripture for his own purposes, the quotes are rarely accurate; the context is ignored, and so the full sense is misconstrued. In this instance Satan omits the words "to keep thee in all thy ways" (KJV). This was the result of a good memory, not a bad one! The omission destroys the truth of the original meaning, which does not encourage the faithful to test God by taking unnecessary risks, but assures believers that God keeps them safe wherever his way leads.

It is dangerous to take portions of Scripture out of the context. The texts can then be used to prove anything, becoming a means of deception. Satan can subtly be the author of a promise-box theology. Promises for the proof of God in our lives can be trusted, but they must be taken in context. Otherwise, God's Word is denied its complete meaning. We are vulnerable to the Tempter's appeal to live by cheap grace, trust easy answers, and seek spectacular solutions.

In regard to this problem, Henri Nouwen points out,

> The temptation to do something spectacular has not lessened since Jesus' days. We all know about the Madison Avenue style of ministry. We do not have to point to the con-men of the cults nor their followers.[4]

It is difficult for people to believe that God would come to visit us in unthreatening and decidedly unspectacular ways: in a manger, in an obscure village, to a humble couple. It has always been difficult for people to believe that things and people of worth can come from unknown places—that God would come as a servant, enter Jerusalem on a donkey, and be executed as a convicted criminal. It is even more difficult to understand how a few unsophisticated fishermen could powerfully proclaim God's message of sovereign grace to the world.

The call to be relevant and spectacular is very subtle. People yield to this temptation because they forget that the final ends and ultimate goals are God-ordained. Didn't Isaiah prophesy that at the name of Jesus every knee should bow and tongue confess (45:23)?

In *Flirting With the World,* John White acutely senses both the immensity and subtlety of the problem:

> The issue is a difficult one because the Christian message should be presented in terms that are relevant to the

> culture in which it is presented. But such a principle may be carried too far. Every Christian enterprise needs a model, and the basic model we have adopted is the entertainment model. Most Christian T.V. shows, whatever positive comments we may make about them, are half hucksterism, half showmanship. From a technical viewpoint the showmanship is often superb. It rivets our attention. . . . We attract people to Jesus by entertaining them. We ignore the truth that Jesus is not a pill needing a sugar coat. . . . He need only to be lifted up, to be manifested. . . . Why do so many professional athletic teams tell Jesus they're trusting him for the win? Does the glory of Christ depend on a victory in a sports stadium? The cutting edge of our evangelism consists all too often of gimmickry and publicity stunts (and bumper stickers such as "I found it!" and "Honk if you love Jesus").[5]

Yes, Satan can and does tempt us in our religious activities and settings. He tempts us to separate the ethics of our methods from the final results. He tempts us to prove ourselves spiritually to others and to test God.

The spectacular will always be "relevant," because our sinful natures childishly crave immediacy, proof, and easy affirmation. To succumb to the temptation for a showy faith is as much a sin as adultery, idolatry, or lying.

Success Sickness

Another way of yielding to the temptation to prove God is to accept the idea that the end justifies the means.

Many practices in our society are "means to an end"—or worse, means without ends. For example, the businessman who takes advantage of a naïve customer but then pays tithes on his profits has given in to temptation in two ways. The TV evangelists, missionaries, or churches who fabricate crisis letters, perhaps exaggerating testimonies, have separated ends from means and therefore have divided God's kingdom.

Jacques Ellul reminds us that

> The first truth which must be remembered is that for Christians there is no disassociation between end and means. . . . Thus, when Jesus Christ is present the Kingdom has "come upon" us. This formula expresses very precisely the relation between the end and the means. Jesus Christ in the incarnation appears as God's means, for the salvation of humankind and for the establishment of the Kingdom of God—the means only appears as the realized presence of the end.[6]

Satan tempted Jesus to use the spectacular, to evangelize without much time or fuss. But it takes time to encounter people in significant ways, as the life and ministry of Jesus revealed afterward. Christ was tempted to build a ministry around a program rather than people and thus make "success" a final goal. Satan tries to make babes of us spiritually and biblically, unable to remember the final approval we are to seek: "Well done, good and faithful servant." Satan tempts us to seek *in this life* a goal of "well done."

Does God call us to be successful in this life? No. We are called to be faithful *and that is success.* Our goal, and the means by which we reach it, is faithfulness. Faithfulness takes time, pain, thought, and a walking by trust rather than sight.

Didn't Jesus realize that there would only be three years of trying ministry? Didn't he know there wouldn't be time for his slow, patient, quiet ministry to one hurt person here, another confused person there? Didn't he know that there was no time to visit Zacchaeus? Jerusalem was waiting! Didn't Jesus realize how painful it would be to start with twelve—eleven of whom would come to sleeping or turning away, and one of whom would betray?

Our society is intoxicated by success. We are addicted

to it. We have our towers of Babel—cities, split-levels, upward mobility—all casting shadows over our spires of worship. Bigger—and farther, and faster—is better. Withdrawal from this addiction can be quite painful, causing fits and convulsions. Let this be the refrain that greets cheap talk of the spectacular: *"Faithfulness is success."*

If you are not sure of the effects of the worship of the spectacular, these words of John White merit attention:

> Does God really get the glory from our evangelism? I do not believe so. You disagree? Think for a minute. How do the media report our campaigns? To whom do they attribute our success? To us. Of course, we may say we give God all the glory, but the world explains the whole thing by pointing to our organizational ability, to our publicity, to our revolutionary technology, to our performing artists, our preachers, and our big names.
>
> But when Jesus was on earth, there were men who gave glory to God as a result of his ministry. As Jesus walked along the Sea of Galilee healing the lame, the blind, the dumb, "the people were amazed. . . . They praised the God of Israel." (Mt. 15:13) Do today's non-Christians react spontaneously in this way? Very rarely. Even when we tell them to give glory to God they respond by admiring us for our spirituality and humility.[7]

This call to worship success is subtle. It is ultimately destructive because it ultimately causes us to test God.

Expand the Facts

Two people we will call John and Mary were involved in a growing successful ministry in a large midwestern church. John was experiencing serious emotional problems. Unfortunately, he denied that the problems existed because he had earlier claimed by faith that they were gone. Life for John was one of personal denial—but the problems remained. A life of spiritual fantasy resulted. John presented an image of a successful ministry but left a trail of disillusioned, hurt, and broken people. His was a life of dishonesty and denial for the sake of keeping up his image. The denial eventually ruined his ministry and tragically fragmented his family.

In the early seventies, a ministry based in Europe had a vision of doing great things for God in the future. In excitement they published articles about a hotel God had given them. Young people from across the United States came to the little village to see this great gift of faith and to be trained for ministry and evangelism. When they arrived, however, the hotel still belonged to the original owner. The group's response to the disillusioned youth was that they had "claimed it by faith." Unfortunately, they published it as though it were fact before it was reality. The owner refused to sell. The group had succumbed to the call of the Evil One and broken God's commandment "You shall not lie."

The temptation to misrepresent ourselves is a call to avoid the pain and process of growth. It is an affliction that can become an epidemic.

Dostoevsky describes this call to Jesus:

> . . . Man cannot bear to be without the miraculous. And as man cannot bear to be without the miraculous, he will create new miracles of his own for himself, and will worship deeds of sorcery and witchcraft, though he might be a hundred times over a rebel, heretic, and infidel. Thou didst not come down from the Cross when they shouted to thee, mocking and reviling thee, "come down from the cross and we will believe that Thou art He." Thou didst not come down, for again Thou wouldst not enslave man by a miracle, and didst crave faith given freely, not based on a miracle.[8]

It is important to understand that basic to the desire for the spectacular and the drive to be relevant is a search for self-affirmation. We need to be seen, praised, admired, appreciated, liked, and accepted. If we don't have realistic understanding of our identity before God, we will have great difficulty when others fail to notice or thank us. In other words, who are we when others fail to recognize us?

Jesus' response to Satan's second temptation is instructive on this point. Christ resisted the temptation to prove God and seek recognition from others. He simply responded to Satan with words from Deuteronomy 6:16: "Do not test the LORD your God." It is futile to see how far we can go with God; there is little good in deliberately placing ourselves into life-threatening situations and then expecting God to come to the rescue. God expects us to take risks in order to be faithful to him. However, faith cannot be dependent on signs and wonders. If faith cannot grow without the spectacular, it is not faith. It is a desire for *sight.*

Rescue Me, God!

How often in times of conflict have we prayed, "If God really loves me, he will give me peace and remove all my obstacles"? How often have we prayed, "Lord, send your power to straighten out my children, my boss, my partner so they will see things as I do"? Or, "God, change these people so that I can really love them"? Aren't these all actually ways of saying, "Prove your love to me by getting me out of this mess?"

What happens when prayers are not answered in the ways we think they should be answered? It may mean there is something intrinsically wrong with the way we have prayed. It should cause us to consider whether we have prayed according to God's will (Matthew 6:10). It may mean that we have been fooled by the temptation to prove God.

Jesus rejected the temptation to follow the Successful, the Spectacular, and the Relevant. To crave the sensational is distrust, not trust. To distrust God is to fail.

Henri Nouwen sees the battle not as one of defeat but as possible victory.

> Our true challenge is to return to the center, to the heart, to the gentle voice that speaks to us and affirms us in a way no human voice ever could. The basis of all life is to be the experience of God's unlimited and unlimiting acceptance of us as beloved children, and acceptance so full, so total, and all embracing that it sets us free to move in the world and act creatively even when we receive little response, even when we are laughed at and rejected, and even when our words and actions lead us to death.[9]

Success is to trust the God who calls us to walk by faith, and to trust God's affirmation of us through the gift of grace. Grace alone frees us from living by the Prove-It and Prove-God principles.

No one is justified in doing evil on the ground of expediency.

—*Theodore Roosevelt*

We have bartered holiness for convenience, loyalty for power, wisdom for information, tradition for fashion.

—*Abraham Heschel*

5.

The Temptation to Expediency

Immediate Power

> Again, the devil took him to a very high mountain and showed him all the kingdoms of the world and their splendor. "All this I will give you," he said, "if you will bow down and worship me."
>
> Jesus said to him, "Away from me, Satan! For it is written: 'Worship the Lord your God, and serve him only' " (Matthew 4:8–10).

Perhaps no culture in history has been so blatantly obsessed with immediate power as our own. This temptation glitters with all the lights of Broadway. Why? Because the call to faithfulness is difficult and risky. How much safer, more satisfying, to acquire things and accept immediate success! How tantalizing the ego! Henri Nouwen identifies the temptation:

> From the moment we present ourselves as the best representative of our grade school class to the moment we try to convince our country that we will be the best possible president, we convince ourselves that the striving for power and want to serve are the same. This fallacy is so deeply ingrained we rarely hesitate to reach for influential positions because we're certain that we do so for the good of the kingdom of God. What good can come

> from powerlessness? In this country of pioneers and self-made achievers, where ambition is praised from the first moment we enter school until we enter the competitive world of free enterprise, we cannot imagine that any good can come from giving up power and or not even desiring it.[1]

Satan's offer of this world's splendor implies that anything of worth must and can be acquired at once. The possession of things, kingdoms, wealth, and power becomes our major proof of success. Those who possess are esteemed, while those who lack are despised. Yet Jesus ignored this obvious chance for visible success and became, instead, the Man of Sorrows, despised and rejected.

When the Tempter's call to live by the Prove-It and Prove-God principles failed, he combined the first two temptations to produce a third that was both spiritual and materialistic.

This last proposition of Satan was the most dangerous and glamorous of all. He took Jesus to the top of a high mountain from which all the kingdoms of the world could be seen. There the Devil explained that these kingdoms were a gift. Jesus could have them, to do with them what he pleased. The only prerequisite was to worship the Devil instead of God.

Jesus was confronted with all the power structures of the world represented in ownership, prestige, status, and esteem. The temptation was to make them the final goal for life. However, they had been promised anyway. So why was this such a great temptation?

The question is not a matter of whether there is something inherently wrong in success, power, money, status, or position. Rather, we must see that Christ was tempted to make them life's ultimate goal. To yield would have made him a materialist and a utilitarian instead of the servant God called him to be.

In this temptation there was also a call to change the world and society by becoming like them, to control the controllers. It invites us to exploit and gain power over others, and it causes us to resent, deny, and resist all forces beyond our control. Why is this call to power and wealth so strong? Sociologist Tony Campolo comments:

> Success is a shining city, a pot of gold at the end of the rainbow. We dream of it as children, we strive for it through our adult lives, and we suffer melancholy in old age if we have not reached it.
>
> Success is the place of happiness. And the anxieties we suffer at the thought of not arriving there gives us ulcers, heart attacks, and nervous disorders. If our reach exceeds our grasp, and we fail to achieve what we want, life seems meaningless and we feel emotionally dead.
>
> Since failure is our unforgivable sin, we are willing to ignore all forms of deviance in people if they just achieve the success symbols which we worship. Therefore, while we send those guilty of petty crimes to penitentiaries, we honor our robber barons by calling them philanthropists and name universities after them.[2]

Success Hides Sin

During my first years in college—the late fifties—the drug culture began to take root in major cities. Great concern was expressed across the country for the tremendous drug-related crime problems in inner cities. When Dave Wilkerson began Teen Challenge in New York, people were overjoyed at this outreach to the crime-ridden drug culture of New York.

Several years later I moved to Europe. By the time I returned to the United States in the seventies, the drug culture had spread to the middle and upper classes. What struck me was that the drug problem was no longer referred to as a crime problem; it was now described as a social problem. Crimes and sins of the affluent are called sociological problems.

People sit by the hours and watch programs like "Love Boat," "Dallas," and "Three's Company," ignoring the absence of moral standards. Why? The stars are doctors, lawyers—the beautiful people. When "Mary Hartman" flashed on the television screen, it was doomed to a short-lived season. I can remember people saying, "How disgusting! It's offensive." Why? The treatment of morals was no different from those on "Love Boat." But Mary Hartman did not eat brunch at Rockefeller Center or dine at the Blue Fox. Her family style was to take pizza home from "Tony's." She would eat in their track-house kitchen. Laundry would be piled on the floor, and empty cereal boxes left on the counter. The stars were not the beautiful people but the fat, the acned, the nervous, the plain, the uneducated. Power, position, and wealth have a way of hiding the reality of sin.

Temptations to Shortcuts

There is still another issue, which reaches far deeper. Satan tempted Jesus to break his relationship with God. He tempted Christ to forsake the God of the ordinary for a god of power and prestige. He tempted Jesus with a beautiful temple rather than a shameful cross surrounded by convicted criminals.

But isn't it the quality that matters? Yes. But quality requires quantity—of time. If you follow the path to Gethsemane, it will demand time. The disciples were not the easiest crowd to work with. "Think of the time you will waste with a few when the whole world is yours," suggested Satan. The worship of God propelled Christ into the pain of relationship.

The temptation to us also is to accept success without a commitment to the time it takes to build relationships. It is a temptation to avoid the risk of rejection. But we must not avoid those relationships that take "too much time" to build.

Many marriages become meaningless because partners demand immediate success. The willingness to take the time required for intimacy is seen as a handicap.

Satan tempts us to accept spirituality without pain, appreciation without rejection, smiles but no tears, blissful disregard rather than righteous anger, applause rather than a crown of thorns. Temptation seldom calls us to a garden of suffering, to spittle in the face, to lashes on our backs, to "a cross to bear." Satan's sales package of spirituality included the avoidance of conflict. How spiritual and expedient this would appear! There would be no need for Jesus to encounter the Romans, the Pharisees, the Sadducees, or the fickle crowds. Rather, he would instantly be king over all the nations.

We all want to take shortcuts. There are quick-and-easy means of food preparation, tax preparation, learning, financial success, and the accumulation of facts. When we attempt to take shortcuts in our spiritual lives because of our fantasies of power and immediate success, we experience the death of all that God created to be meaningful. Satan tempts us to focus on and fantasize ends and then look for shortcut means.

When life presses in on our families, Satan may take us to a high mountain to focus on what could have been, or what it would have been like: "If only I had married that person, or taken that job, or moved there." "I wish my children were like the Smiths'." These kinds of fantasies sabotage the most meaningful relationships God intended for us to experience.

When we succumb to these fantasies, we crush all that could be meaningful and beautiful. Congregations can attack pastors because they haven't brought immediate success. Parents can be tempted to resent each other or their children because they haven't lived up to their visions of the ideal marriage and family. Our goals, like the promise of the kingdom made to Christ, are usually God-given. However, the Tempter calls us to be expedient. He tempts us, as he tempted our Lord, to sidestep the time and pain it takes to build character and relationships.

Understanding Idolatry

The temptation to expediency also involves idolatry. The invitation to idolatry lies at the core of all the temptations of Jesus. During a visit to the Caribbean, I was fascinated by a group of tourists laughing at a man selling hand-carved gods on the beach. As enlightened people, they readily regarded this kind of idol worship as stupid. However, I believe the tourists were unenlightened to the fact that our society has largely followed the Tempter's call to become idol worshipers. We may be the greatest image-making society the world has ever known. Images are peddled in every facet of our culture.

Politicians hire image makers who are skillful at carving images for the masses to embrace, in the same way that Satan tempted Jesus to seduce the crowds. An image represents something else. It is carbon copied and word processed to remove all flaws. Images may or may not relate to the reality of the person or product they represent. Because we do not know the politicians personally, we have little way of judging the genuineness of the carvings. We are at the mercy of the beachside craftsmen selling their goods.

We also worship the gods of wealth, glamor, power, beauty, and popularity because of the temptations of the image makers. Sometimes the gods are called celebrities. Their values are unimportant; their morality as well. But we worship them and help to make them wealthy because they have captured the attention of the public.

There's a MAIDS disease in our society—Moral Acquired Immune Deficiency Syndrome. Unknowingly our gods can carry this disease for years, infect others through social contact, and cause them to lose their moral sensitivity and integrity. Symptomatic of MAIDS is the tendency to judge others on the basis of popularity rather than on personal character, integrity, and ethics. The worship of celebrities has caused us to lose moral sensitivity.

Barbara Goldsmith penned these words in a column in the *New York Times.*

> At a recent Manhattan dinner party, the celebrity guests included a United States senator, an embezzler, a woman rumored to have spent $60,000 a year on flowers, a talk show host, the chief executive officer of one of America's largest corporations, a writer who had settled a plagiarism suit and a Nobel laureate. There was once a day when you couldn't have gotten together a group such as that; but today you can because we are in love with celebrities, for whatever reason. The line between fame and notoriety has been erased. Today we are faced with a vast confusing jumble of celebrities—the talented, the untalented, heroes and villains, people of accomplishment and those who have accomplished nothing at all. The criterion for their celebrity being is that their image encapsulates some form of the American dream. They give enough of appearance of leadership, heroism, wealth, success, power, glamor, excitement to feed our fantasies. We no longer demand reality, only that which is real seemingly. Synthetic celebrities are our own creation. The modern equivalent of biblical graven images. Bowing down to them we absent ourselves from the everyday ethical and moral judgments that insure the health of society.[3]

This is a poignant condemnation of the society in which we live today. Unlike Jesus, who didn't bow, we have bowed prostrate to the gods of fantasy rather than embracing reality. In choosing fantasy over reality, we trivialize life, defining it according to what feels good and looks successful.

Several years ago the TV series "Dallas" had a special segment entitled "Who Shot J. R.?" Following the telecast, a Boston station gave ten minutes of news time to interviews with people in local bars as to their opinions regarding who shot J. R. Ewing. The station devoted less than one minute to reporting the brutal beating murder of an elderly person that had happened the same day.

In 1984 the media and the public were outraged by the careless use of the word *cripple* in a public statement by then-Secretary of the Interior James Watt. However, the State of Indiana granted permission for a young couple to perform infanticide on their handicapped nine-month-old child by withholding life-sustaining medical treatment. There was no large public outcry and there was little coverage by the media.

The film *The Day After,* which depicts what might happen in the case of nuclear war, was shown on TV amid great controversy. The stated purpose was to marshal public support for a governmental freeze on nuclear weapons. The strongest result was that many people took Valium or sought counseling because of the fear of what might happen if the staged production were to become a reality. Yet few go to counseling, speak out, or take Valium over the fact that 1.5 million infants are being terminated annually through abortion.

Idolatry leads to a preference for fantasy over reality, for worshiping the created rather than the Creator. Has not the church, like the world, yielded to idolatry also, following the gods of success, popularity, and good feelings?

I was invited to speak in the chapel of a prominent Christian college, and my topic was "The Character of God and Personal Conversion." Prior to the sermon, the captain of the soccer team ran onto the platform and ate a raw potato while singing "Jesus Loves Me." He had promised to do this if the soccer team won its game the day before.

This kind of buffoonery happens, perhaps in less obvious ways, in churches also. Shortly after I gave that chapel sermon, I attended a conference on worship. The topic of discussion was "How can we make our people happy with worship?" The discussion went on for hours, evoking comments such as "Some like folk music, others classical, some want informal services, and some formal. So what do we do?" The clergymen in attendance would have died a martyr's death for their belief in the authority of Scripture. But never was the question asked, "What does Scripture say about worship?" or "Who is this God we worship?" The focus was on people, their feelings, and their folksiness.

It is the trivializing of worship—the human-centered, clichéd prayers, unedifying announcements, experience-centered gospel songs—that has made us victims of the image makers in our society. We must remind ourselves that we are not to be worshiping our "best buddy." God, our Creator and our Judge, demands our worship. Not to worship this God will expose us to the call of the Evil One to bow down to success, fantasy, popularity, and power. This God has provided only one image to worship: Jesus Christ. Jesus is the only refuge that can protect us from bowing down to the image makers of our age who carve their gods, not in wood or stone, but in our minds.

Preserve Your Power

Idolatry is the basic temptation that causes us to abuse power. It is the thing that's wrong with power struggles. Whenever we succumb to the temptation to enter a power struggle, whether in diplomacy, in business, or in our families, someone ends up being hurt or destroyed. Whether it involves two children fighting over the bigger piece of the apple or nations stockpiling arms, most power struggles end in destructiveness in some form.

This temptation faces us each day of our lives. We are tempted, as Christ was, to focus on the external marks of success, sidestep ethical issues, and avoid the pain of relationships. There is a tension between God's truth and our instinct for self-preservation. Basically it is an issue of appearance. We are tempted to appear to be right even if that conflicts with being right. Didn't Jesus know that because he disregarded appearances, many would view him as a failure?

The temptation to appear right pressures people to justify decisions through rationalization and manipulation. Satan tempts us to use God-given positions of power to protect our appearances in the sight of others. It's subtle, but it's always there. We all struggle daily against the urge to make decisions out of pure emotion, blind assumptions, and selfish interest. This temptation causes us to defend or deny our weaknesses, failures, and mistakes. It crushes the truth. When truth is crushed, power corrupts.

The Tempter corrupts us by tempting us to be more concerned about preserving our positions than following God's will. "I will give you these kingdoms," is the call.

Any position in life can give us the illusion of security. Satan tempts us to find security in position rather than in God. Why? Because God's ways are often too costly for us.

Pontius Pilate offers a fitting example of one who faced this battle. In his dialogue with Jesus Christ he faced the same pressures we face daily—to believe in rumor rather than fact, to use a God-entrusted position of authority for self-preservation, to choose immediate security rather than the benefits of truth, to separate our positions of power from the facts.

Pilate had to choose between two options. He chose to preserve his finite power and believe rumor and false accusations. He chose the security of the immediate rather than the long-term benefits of the truth. The pursuit of truth was too costly. At that point, his position of power became corrupt. When the conscious decision is made to believe rumor, as did Pilate, sarcastic responses become the only defense for preservation of power. "What is truth?" was Pilate's response. If he had really wanted to find out, he would have stayed and continued the dialogue.

We all have struggles with power, from the tiny baby to the controlling dictator. The major issue facing us is how to use a position of power to pursue the truth. When we bypass truth to preserve our positions of power, we find that power corrupts. It is only when we honor the truth that we discover it is the greatest power in the world.

Jesus refused the temptation to gain instant power over people. When he fed the multitude, the enthusiasm of the crowds began a campaign to "make him king" (John 6:15). Jesus escaped to the hills to find solitude. From the first day of ministry to the last moments on the cross, Christ refused to give in to the lure of personal success.

To give in to the temptation to expediency is tantamount to embracing cruelty, ruthlessness, force, and hate. The universal drive for domination all too often replaces the Christ-appointed task of serving men and women to the point of self-sacrifice and suffering.

Worship and Service Are Necessary

How will we know when we are beginning to succumb to these basic temptations? There are two ways. First, our devotion and worship of Christ will diminish and we will be more inclined to worship material and nonspiritual things. Second, our devotion to others will diminish. Jesus' response to Satan's temptation touched on both these matters.

> Jesus said to him, "Away from me, Satan! For it is written: 'Worship the Lord your God, and serve him only' " (Matthew 4:10).

Jesus linked worship and service in his response to Satan. Satan appeals to us to take the route of expediency and control. Jesus responds with an affirmation of relationship—relationship with God through worship, and relationship with others through service. God's kingdom is not characterized by impersonal power. The great wonder of Jesus' work was not the miracles he performed, but his refusal to abuse the power in his hands. Being God in human form, Christ could have taken all the kingdoms of the world with one little breath. He chose instead to veil power in gentleness, caring, compassion, worship, and service. Why? Because God's purpose is not to control, to dazzle, to invoke the spectacular; rather, he has come to seek, to affirm, and to serve.

Jesus refused the temptation to expediency on the ground that only God should be worshiped and served.

Henri Nouwen sees this issue as foundational to most temptation:

> A world that worships power, and sees it as an ultimate mark of success, has a hard time comprehending a kind of success that is based on the mutual submission of love.[4]

If we worship God and seek to be controlled by his will, we can learn to use our wealth, power, and prestige for the service of others.

The great mystery of ministry that Jesus modeled for us is a call, not to worship power, but to serve God in powerlessness.

When tempted to abuse power, Jesus responded by saying, "You must worship the Lord your God and serve him alone." These words are reminders that only undivided attention to God Almighty can stem our desire for expediency and power. Without this foundation we will be tempted to be self-seeking, manipulative, and violent even as we deceive ourselves into believing that these are all for the sake of ministry. We dress up our power in clichés and robes of humility. We delude ourselves into believing we are serving while actually we are protecting our own interests.

Even in the church, Satan may call us to pit ourselves against others with idealistic affirmations that we are being "faithful to God's truth." While willfully blind to our own craftiness and hankering for power, we vainly use God's name to justify our actions. This temptation is strong because our society is competitive. The Tempter says, "You are nothing if you are not productive."

Jesus faced the very temptations that you and I face daily, temptations that rip us apart. He understands the pain, the hurt, the fears. How? Because he has been there. He stood against sensationalism and success, choosing rather to come down from the mountain in order to serve people—even if that meant the Cross.

Satan has patience, however. He knows how to wait. The offers that Jesus refused have found takers who have had themselves crowned in his place. For the Lord, the path led to the final paradox of death on a cross between two thieves. That is the ultimate extreme of God's love for humankind. Christ identified with our struggles, hurts, despair, temptations—and with our death and victory.

In light of eternal judgment, he who refuses to forgive others breaks down the bridge over which he himself must pass, for everyone has need to be forgiven.

—*Bishop Fulton Sheen*

God calls us to have reverence for our personalities and our enemies.

—*E. Stanley Jones*

6.

The Temptation to Reject Forgiveness

A Benefit of the Faith

I once heard a retired psychologist say, "The benefits of the Christian faith are to be found in the understanding of forgiveness." Daily we walk in a world that can mark us with hurts, pain, discouragement, and rejection. Tensions may attack the very foundation of our emotional and spiritual stability. These hurts, unexpected tragedies, and pressures will inevitably lead us into situations in which we must give or ask for forgiveness. David Augsburger writes,

> No relationship exists long without tensions. No community continues long without conflicts. No human interaction occurs without the possibility of pain, injury, suffering, and alienation. The hurts are always there. The misunderstandings inevitably happen. There is invariably trouble. Without forgiveness, community is only possible where people are superficial.
>
> With forgiveness, we are set free to meet genuinely, to interact authentically, to risk being fully present with each other in integrity. Such forgiveness draws people toward each other. It comes to terms with the past, then allows it to be truly past. It opens the future but does not determine it so that people are unable to be living, free

and spontaneous again. It deals clearly with the present in true repentance, change and growth.[1]

Most Christians can agree with this statement, but find the act of forgiving difficult. Have you ever asked yourself why people allow resentments to remain in the archives of their minds? What makes couples hold on to hurts for years and then suddenly explode, sending their families into chaos and confusion? What is it in our lives that will make us join a peace march, give to the poor, support missionaries, and lead others to Christ, yet succumb to the temptation to refuse to forgive those closest to us? Why do we struggle, in fact, to forgive ourselves? Is it that we fail to see this as a battle with temptation?

Forgiveness is the greatest gift we can give one another. To withhold it is an act of cruelty and sin. C. S. Lewis saw this as a basic spiritual battle.

> Everyone says forgiveness is a lovely idea, until they have something to forgive, as we had during the war. And then, to mention the subject at all is to be greeted with howls of anger. It is not that people think this too high and difficult a virtue; it is that they think it hateful and contemptible.[2]

It is the willingness or unwillingness to grant forgiveness that reveals our true stance with God.

Why does Satan tempt us to refuse the gift of forgiveness? Simply, to accept it or to grant it is to give up control. This control becomes a deadly weapon used to terrify and threaten relationships.

I was talking once with a young man whose life has been dedicated to the fight against nuclear arms buildup (a position with which I personally concur). During the conversation I raised several issues concerning his relationship with his parents. Suddenly there was an explosion of hostility and bitterness. "I haven't even contacted those rednecks for over a year," he said. I agree that his parents hadn't been the best of models.

However, I knew them, and I knew how much they longed to have a relationship with their son.

What makes a young man willing to leave a promising profession, risk personal freedom, spend hours researching to fight the possible annihilation of the human race, and yet refuse to forgive his parents? His refusal to forgive was a weapon of sin and control, and Satan was having a heyday in his life. None of us is immune to this temptation.

Self-Hate May Be Pride

A young woman I'll call Pamela talked with me about her inability to forgive herself. Her mother passed away during her last year of graduate school at Harvard. Her mother's death severed a very deep and unique relationship, the kind most mothers and daughters dream of having. Pam faced normal grieving coupled with feelings of bitterness, anger, and hurt. When support from others was needed, she received only spiritual platitudes rather than genuine care. In frustration she sought a new beginning in Florida. She was a part of the jet-set crowd in Miami in a matter of months. While seeking the friendships and support she needed, she ended up with a string of broken relationships, sexual encounters, an illegitimate child, and a crushed self-image. Returning to the Northeast, she eventually married and became involved in a church. However, she couldn't resolve her guilt and forgive herself. Her past experiences became a mental and spiritual prison. She felt worthless and had difficulty developing significant relationships with others. She rejected God's forgiveness because she saw herself as worthless.

What makes people unable to forgive themselves? Why do they lock themselves into prisons of self-hate? In simple terms, they fail to see that rejection of God's forgiveness and refusal to grant it to others are both acts of sin.

At the core of Pam's problem was a temptation to pride. She was declaring in effect, "God, your Word says you forgive me unconditionally, including my past failures. But your decision to forgive me is wrong." Isn't that the heart of the matter? Satan tempts us to accept forgiveness on our own terms; that way we lose no control over our self-hate. In turn, Satan tempts us to withhold forgiveness from others so we can cling to our position of control over them.

Forgiveness was at the center of our Lord's teaching. It often caused deep distress to those who heard it. Peter was troubled by Jesus' teaching about forgiveness. How could anyone forgive so completely? Finally he came to Jesus and asked, "Lord, how many times shall I forgive my brother when he sins against me? Up to seven times?" (Matthew 18:21). Now, seven is not a very large number. But could any of us honestly forgive another for the same insult seven times? Unforgiveness is not a trivial offense. Isn't the central temptation the desire to control the offender?

Hear what Jesus says: "I tell you, not seven times, but seventy-seven times" (v. 22).

Forgiveness is the central theme of Scripture. Perhaps we need to examine the subject more clearly to avoid the same sin as the young man and woman. Both were enslaved by their refusal to forgive. They couldn't release their weapons of vindictive control over self or others. They failed to see this attitude as sinful. The fact is, all of us are tempted to be unforgiving of ourselves and others in varying degrees.[3]

Resisting God's Grace

To deny forgiveness is to refuse to allow Christ's character to reign in us. To deny forgiveness is to oppose relationships—our relationships with God, others, and self. It is the way of the Tempter, Satan. The young man and woman were both in rebellion. They were victimized by temptation and didn't realize it. This temptation attacks the very core of God's kingdom of justice, care, concern, and love; it's the rejection of the Cross.

John considered the issue central. "Since God so loved us, we also ought to love one another" (1 John 4:11). What allows us to experience that love? "If we confess our sins," John writes, "he is faithful and just and will forgive us our sins and purify us from all unrighteousness" (1 John 1:9). Many struggles result directly from a misunderstanding of confession and forgiveness. We can tread paths of isolation, fight unnecessary battles, and face alienation simply because we misunderstand the impact that confession and forgiveness can make on our lives.

Confession and Forgiveness

What is confession? What is forgiveness? John says that confession precedes but is coupled with forgiveness.

Many things that pass for confession have little to do with the apostles' teaching on the subject. Judas' experience demonstrates a confused understanding of confession.

> When Judas, who had betrayed him, saw that Jesus was condemned, he was seized with remorse and returned the thirty silver coins to the chief priests and elders. "I have sinned," he said, "for I have betrayed innocent blood."
>
> "What is that to us?" they replied. "That's your responsibility."
>
> So Judas threw the money into the temple and left. Then he went away and hanged himself (Matthew 27:3–5).

Confession is not just being sorry for our wrongs. Judas was sorry. Confession is not merely discussing wrongs with religious leaders. Judas did that as well.

Judas felt sorrow, experienced remorse, and confessed. However, his confession brought no release. Like many of us, he went to the religious leaders to plead his case rather than going to God. He even returned the money. But neither his confession nor his return of the money brought release from his emotional torment. Judas' self-hatred led to self-destruction.

If discussing our sins were the same as confession, then the last couple of decades have certainly been confessing years. Ever since the free speech crisis at Berkeley in 1964, we have let it all come out, without reservation. Nevertheless, our generation is on a road to cultural suicide. Various encounter groups, thousands of talk shows, and hundreds of articles encourage people to let it all hang out. Seldom, however, are people encouraged to say, "I have sinned against God, my neighbor, my wife, my parents. I need forgiveness." Encounter groups, counseling sessions, and discussions with friends may be good and needed therapy, but they are not confession.

Confession is not just getting things out and explained. Judas pointed to his wrongdoing: "I have betrayed innocent blood." Judas explained and admitted sin, but there was no relief.

The Desire to Explain

We are all experts at explaining things. Our expertise begins at an early age. I was reminded of this fact when I was nineteen and was baby-sitting my two-and-a-half-year-old nephew for the first time. Dennis entered the house covered from head to foot with mud. Asked how he became so dirty, he quickly explained that his toy wooden duck had pushed him in the mud puddle. He was convinced that I would buy his explanation and excuse him. The punch line came when he said, "It was the toy duck you gave me."

Satan tempts us to explain things. "If you just understood my need for affection, you would excuse my uncontrolled passions." "If you understood, you would see that I am a victim of circumstances." Explaining feelings or circumstances is not confession; it is usually a rationalization to avoid confession and forgiveness.

In the biblical view, secret sins are to be dealt with secretly. We have the freedom and are encouraged to keep some confessions between ourselves and God. Scripture not only protects privacy, but protects interpersonal problems from becoming tools of exploitation. Sins against another person are to be addressed only with that person and with careful consideration for that person's vulnerabilities. If the issues cannot be resolved privately, then and only then should the problem be brought before mediators.

> If your brother sins against you, go and show him his fault, just between the two of you. If he listens to you, you have won your brother over. But if he will not listen, take one or two others along, so that "every matter may be established by the testimony of two or three witnesses." If he refuses to listen to them, tell it to the church; and if he refuses to listen even to the church, treat him as you would a pagan or a tax collector (Matthew 18:15–17).

When someone wrongs us, God calls us to contact that person individually, not the congregation or even another friend. We are asked to walk down a private road, not a public thoroughfare.

If difficulties arise or sins are committed against a group or community, the scriptural model calls for confessing and dealing with the problem in the group. Paul publicly challenged Peter in Antioch when Peter followed the Galatians into legalistic enslavement (see Galatians 2:11 and Acts 15). His example can serve as a guideline for group confrontation and submission. To forgive assumes a confession and admission of a wrong. Do you see why Satan drives us into explaining?

Not only are we to keep the categories in proper perspective, but we must address other issues around confession. All of us are victimized by various situations and circumstances beyond our control. We cannot deny that to a certain extent, we are products of environment and of genetic and psychological conditioning. We must still accept responsibility, however, for what we do. Why? Because sin is where we go wrong—beyond any question of determinist factors.

Coupled with confession, remorse is good. But again we ask, In whose direction? Judas had remorse but was expressing it to the wrong people. It was good therapy, but brought no release.

We do not feel remorse unless we realize how much pain we inflict on others who are made in God's image. Confession to the right person without remorse is not a biblical confession. Ray Stedman tells of a qualified remorse:

> I once read of a man who wrote a letter to the Bureau of Internal Revenue saying, "I haven't been able to sleep because last year, when I filled out my income tax report, I deliberately misrepresented my income. I am enclosing a check for $150, and if I still can't sleep, I will send you the rest.[4]

When the crunch comes, Satan tempts us to explain things and to sidestep full responsibility. True confession accepts full responsibility for both actions and consequences with the goal of reconciliation—not the goal of relieving sleepless nights.

Forgiveness is not excusing. In his booklet *Forgiveness* Dan Hamilton writes,

> A valid excuse eliminates the need for forgiveness. Consider the man who was driving his new car home. Along a country road, a small girl appeared from the weeds and threw a rock through the side window. The man pulled his car off the road and ran back to catch the kid and administer some instant justice. But she hadn't run away. She just waited there, and said, "I am sorry I hit your car, mister, but I had to. My little brother is hurt and

there's no one here to help." That's the effect of a good excuse. What we first saw as punishable sin we now see as a necessary allowable act under the circumstances.

Every action has a reason behind it, but not every reason is an excuse. That which we can excuse we need not forgive; only that which we cannot excuse is in need of forgiveness. *God forgives because God does not excuse everything.*[5]

Forgiving is not making allowances for others. God calls us to forgive people's faults and sins—not to overlook them. When we yield to the temptation to overlook sin we do a great disservice to the person contending with sin.

> In light of the eternal judgment, he who refuses to forgive others breaks down the bridge over which he himself must pass, for everyone has need to be forgiven. The divine Law is that only those who forgive will be forgiven. It is much easier to forgive the weak who have injured us or those who are beneath us in dignity than it is to forgive the powerful or the better or nobler whom we have injured. It will generally be found that when the person who has been injured is nobler than oneself, a deep resentment often follows.[6]

Not to Forgive Is to Hold Power

At the core of our unwillingness to forgive is a desire to have power over others. To overlook their sins is equally as controlling. Why are we so willing to forgive our children and not our supervisors? Why do professors willingly forgive students but resist forgiving administrators? What makes us nurture former hurts inflicted by superiors while we're willing to forgive those inflicted by subordinates? It is because we fail to see these issues as battles with temptation and sin.

We usually do not request—or grant—forgiveness for things that do not hurt. A person can normally forgive things that have caused pain. It is easier for us to discuss forgiving Hitler, Marx, or Nixon or another public figure who has never marked our lives than it is to forgive a friend who has directly wronged us. The former is rummage-sale forgiveness; the latter—true forgiveness—requires that we release our control.

One beautiful Sunday afternoon in August, our family went to the ocean to have a picnic, as we often do. Our son, Bradford, five at the time, slid down a grassy slope, imprinting indelible grass stains on his Sunday slacks. My immediate response was anger. For some reason, this incident unleashed some pent-up anger, and he became the focus of a furious outburst. I went beyond the point of correcting, even though I could see the hurt in his eyes. My daughter, Monique, age nine at the time, looked at me tearfully and said, "Daddy, your relationship with Bradford is more important than any ol' grass stains." Her words cut to the core. Like a surgeon's scalpel, they uncovered a malignant attitude that was alienating me from Bradford. All of us in the family felt the pain and hurt inflicted by my sin. When I asked Bradford's forgiveness, he embraced me, saying, "I love you, Daddy." That was forgiveness born of personal pain.

Attack Problems—Not People

All human forgiveness is to be founded upon God's forgiveness expressed in Christ. Our willingness to forgive follows from the assurance of God's forgiveness. Is our difficulty with forgiving rooted in blindness to our own sins and a refusal to accept Christ's love? Satan tempts us to use our unchecked sins to weave other people into neurotic and pathological webs.

God's goal for us is to attack problems rather than people. This is not easy to do. C. S. Lewis faced this struggle.

> I remember Christian teachers telling me long ago that I must hate a bad man's actions, but not hate the bad man. They would say, hate the sin but not the sinner.
>
> For a long time I used to think this a silly, straw-splitting distinction; how could you hate what one did and not hate the person? But years later it occurred to me that there was one man to whom I had been doing this all my life—namely myself. However much I might dislike my own cowardice or conceit or greed, I went on loving myself. There had never been the slightest difficulty about it. In fact, I hated the things precisely because I loved the man. Just because I was sorry to find that I was the sort of man who did those things. Consequently, Christianity does not want us to reduce by one atom the hatred we feel for cruelty and treachery. We ought to hate them.[7]

This attitude enables people to forgive others and themselves and yet not overlook faults and sins.

We do not understand forgiveness entirely, however, if we fail to acknowledge that there are times when forgiveness itself is an act of control. It can be used as a weapon against those weaker than we. This is yet another form of the temptation to the sin of control. David Augsburger writes,

> When forgiveness puts you in a one-up position, care enough not to forgive. One-up forgiveness is an emotion which exists solely in connection with judgment and condemnation. . . .
>
> To say, "I forgive you," can mean "I have examined, weighed, judged you and your behavior and found you sorely lacking in qualities that are worthy of my respect. I have these qualities at this point in time, but you do not. I humbly recognize my superior moral strength and your weakness, my consistent moral behavior and your inconsistency or immorality. I forgive your trespasses. We will henceforth have a relationship based on the recognition of my benevolence in the hour of your neediness, my generosity in the fact of your guilt. You will find some

suitable way to be dutifully grateful from this day forward."[8]

It is a subtle yet powerful truth: Keeping control does not allow biblical forgiveness; biblical forgiveness leaves no room for the sin of control.

Giving Up Our Weapons

Do you ever wonder why Satan wreaks such confusion with this issue of forgiving? Put in simple terms, *Forgiving causes us to lose our weapons of control.* At the same time, the Evil One loses control over us when we forgive! We lose the power to inflict pain on others and ourselves to prevent growth and foster hurts. Dan Hamilton observes,

> People get ulcers not from what they eat, but from what eats them. If we insist on the pleasure of hatred, we forfeit all the things that make life worth living. . . . We undermine the gospel when we fail to forgive. Our refusal to forgive tells the world much about us. It says that we're hardhearted because we won't give others the gift we have received. We quench our thirst for justice, selfishly, before we meet another person's basic needs. Ungratefully, we forget how much we have already been forgiven (Matthew 18:21–35). We will not allow faults in other people, while we ourselves are imperfect (Luke 6:41–42; John 8:1–11).[9]

Satan tempts us to reflect his character rather than God's. God calls us to forgive and love others in the same way we have been loved. Hamilton says, "God does not love any of us for our nice, attractive qualities which we think we possess, but just because we are the things called selves."[10]

Evil Has Limits

We live in God's universe. All evil and temptation function within the boundaries of cause and effect. Evil breeds more evil. Bitterness gives birth to more bitterness. Temptation entertained inculcates increased vulnerability to temptation. Likewise, goodness generates goodness. Obedience encourages more obedience. Forgiveness generates additional forgiveness. Character encourages character. God has created us in such a way that the choices we make today largely determine what our character will be ten years from now.

Character development and maturity do not happen automatically with the graying of one's hair. No! There is a process that begins with the decisions and choices made today. We are called to reflect God's character today and every day.

Here is the primary motivation for forgiving: Forgiveness is a part of God's character. As we see God's character revealed in Scripture, we will be filled with a desire to emulate him.

In Exodus 34, for example, we read: "[The Lord] passed in front of Moses, proclaiming, 'The LORD, the LORD, the compassionate and gracious God, slow to anger, abounding in love and faithfulness, maintaining love to thousands, and forgiving wickedness, rebellion and sin' " (vv. 6–7).

John Stott says,

> Forgiveness is indispensable to the life and health of the soul as food is for the body. So the next prayer [speaking of the Lord's Prayer] is, Forgive our debts. Sin is likened to a "debt" because it deserves to be punished. But when God forgives sin, he remits the penalty and drops the charge against us. The addition of the words "as we also have forgiven our debtors" is further emphasized in verses 14 and 15 which follow the prayer and state that our Father will forgive us if we forgive others but will not forgive us if we refuse to forgive others. This certainly

> does not mean that our forgiveness of others earns us the right to be forgiven. It is rather that God forgives only the penitent and that one of the chief evidences of true penitence is a forgiving spirit.[11]

Satan subtly tempts us to hold an exaggerated view of others' offenses, thereby minimizing our own.

God takes seriously the worth of our neighbors, the people we have shunned off as second class to avoid responsible care and love. The discovery of God's love for us ignites discovery of our neighbors' worth. Jay Adams calls this *the act of redemptive forgiveness.*[12] This is forgiveness that reflects the forgiveness of God. Not only love for God, but all Christian love is reciprocal: "We love because he first loved us" (1 John 4:19).

To build on this foundation is to destroy old walls we have built between ourselves and those we have written off. We can then say, "I want to be your friend again." "I want to be your son again." "Let's enter into a new relationship together and begin again."

Francis Schaeffer addressed the issue in his book *The Mark of the Christian.* "What is the final apologetic? . . . The love that true Christians show for each other and not just for their own party."[13]

> A new command I give you: Love one another. As I have loved you, so you must love one another. *By this all men will know that you are my disciples, if you love one another* (John 13:34–35, italics mine).

Do you ever feel that you cannot forgive? If so, that is a temptation to sin. You are being tempted to use your hurts, hate, and resentment as a weapon against other human beings.

When we respond to Satan's call, he binds us in a strait jacket of resentment and makes us slaves to revenge. All of us can be shackled to memories of pain and hurt. Or we can be held by our past sins. Like a video tapedeck stuck on permanent replay, the mind can rerun again and again the hurtful things done in the past.

Power Comes From Accepting God's Grace

How do we overcome the temptation to be unforgiving? Do we overcome by thinking positive thoughts about others? No, that will not be sufficient. The power to forgive comes by accepting God's forgiveness.

Forgiving helps us take steps toward nurturing relationships rather than building bastions of cynicism centered around resentment.

The only thing God cannot forgive is our rejection of his forgiveness. God honors our choices. When we fail to show forgiveness to others we reveal to the world outside our response to God's love.

Paul encouraged the church in Ephesus to

> Be kind to one another, tenderhearted, *forgiving* one another, as God in Christ *forgave* you. Therefore be *imitators* of God, as beloved children. And walk in love, as Christ loved us and gave himself up for us, a fragrant offering and sacrifice to God (Ephesians 4:32–5:2 RSV, italics mine).

Paul gives instructions for kindness, because forgiving is not natural. Like unbelievers, Christians are tempted to be unkind, hurtful, and unforgiving. But by God's grace, we are to reveal God to the world by our character. We are to imitate God. This just echoes the opening chapters of Genesis. Men and women are made in the image of God. We are to reflect God's character—that which we were originally created to do and be. The world is to be drawn to God not by our perfection, orthodoxy or absence of difficulties but by our forgiveness expressed to others. We witness to the world our need for God's grace when we forgive each other.

"If we confess our sins, he is faithful and just to forgive us our sins and cleanse us from all unrighteousness." Jesus Christ frees us to take new steps toward maturity.

Forgiveness ignites love where love was previously nonexistent. Forgiveness imitates God's way of dealing with people: "While we were yet sinners, Christ died for our sins."

People forgive as they love. Since God loves infinitely, God forgives without limit. God's choice to forgive, and ours, provides the healing power for living well.

No man, for any considerable period, can wear one face to himself, and another to the multitude, without finally getting bewildered as to which may be the true.

—*Nathaniel Hawthorne*

God's grace resounds in our lives like a staccato. Only by retaining the seemingly disconnected notes comes the ability to grasp the theme.

—*Abraham Heschel*

7.

Seeing Yourself Through the Eyes of God

Guilt Causes Problems

Does Satan ever tempt you to feel that because you struggle with a besetting sin or temptation, you cannot be useful to God? Are you ever tempted to judge others because their Christian experience doesn't seem quite as alive as yours? Or does the Evil One get you discouraged because you don't live up to your own expectations of spirituality? Do you ever struggle with feelings of low self-esteem or despair?

If any of these questions strikes a responsive chord, then Satan is probably tempting you to live under the burden of unresolved guilt. This burden is one of the most destructive forces known to humankind.

Guilt can lead to bizarre behavior while causing tremendous problems with self-acceptance. It disables us from relating to and serving others. Most tragically, it makes us vulnerable to the manipulative tactics of other people. Numerous parents know instinctively that the best way to hold control over their children is to make them feel guilty. Psychologist Mario Jacoby writes,

> They [parents] appeal to their guilt feelings, directly or indirectly. "Look how lonely I am." "Look how I love you

and do everything for you." "Look how I suffer, and how helpless I am."[1]

Almost without realizing it, parents can be tempted to use guilt to control, never envisioning the long-range damage this can have on children.

Satan has used everything from religious hucksters to totalitarian governments to manipulate people by appeal to embedded guilt. Jacoby says, "Totalitarian states have special propaganda ministers who turn and twist the facts until they can convince the population that the decisions and the cause of the dictator are just and justified."[2] To disagree, therefore, is to be "guilty" of injustice. Whether Satan uses a totalitarian state, religious leader, or patronizing parent, he victimizes people usually by appealing to their guilt feelings.

Unresolved guilt can disable us spiritually, psychologically, and emotionally. Alfred Adler concluded that guilt can pressure a person to adopt exaggerated goals of self-enchantment, causing serious problems with insecurity and inferiority complexes. Guilt may drive a person to live in a fantasy world to avoid facing reality. Adler writes,

> The neurotic takes it [the fantasy] literally, and the psychotic attempts its realization. . . .
>
> Guilt can also serve in the interest of gaining distance, that is, withdrawing. . . . Since all forms of behavior are in the service of the goal to be attained, it is indeed possible that guilt . . . may be used for withdrawing and at another time for aggression, or for both purposes simultaneously. Preference for the hinterland of life is notably safeguarded by the individual's mode of thinking, or by fruitless guilt feelings. . . . Groundless self-accusation on account of masturbation, for example, supplies a suitable pretext for practicing it. Looking back on his past everyone would like to have many things undone. But in the case of the neurotic such regrets serve as an excellent excuse for not cooperating.[3]

I know several people who have left productive and rewarding professions to follow what they felt was a call from God, purely as a means of trying to mitigate unresolved guilt. Satan tempts us to victimize ourselves with feelings of guilt brought by his accusations: "I haven't been reading my Bible enough." "I am a terrible parent." "I shouldn't be having these questions." "I am such a failure as a marriage partner (or pastor or mother or Christian)."

Satan tempts us to heap guilt upon more guilt until we are buried under a rubble of depression, internalized anger, frustrations, and feelings of worthlessness. How does one get out? Is there any way of escape? When is guilt a result of the Holy Spirit's work in our lives, and when a result of the Tempter's attack?

"If you were the captain of an invading army, you would find the weakest spot in your opponent's defenses and go for the kill," writes Hal Lindsey.[4] That area of vulnerability for the believer, Satan knows, is guilt. We all deal with guilt in various ways.

Satan often tempts us to deny guilt. Denial may result in various forms of compensatory behavior. We can overwork. Bishop Sheen noted that "George Bernard Shaw once said that modern man is too busy to think about his sins."[5] Westerners are known for "doing business." Activities can be a means to avoidance, especially from ourselves. Turning on the stereo, TV, or radio can also be avoidance. We drown out our inner selves and struggles while temptation comes to excuse us. "Oh, I really didn't mean that." "It was just a white lie." "We all slip at times." "You know what can happen when you are lonely."

Excused Actions Intensify Guilt

People who excuse their actions only intensify their guilt. In reality, Satan never deceives us successfully. We know inside how wrong, destructive, and vindictive we have been in thought, word, and deed. The by-product? More difficulties with acceptance of self and others—a prime target for Satan's attack. Denial and excuses add building blocks to the shaky foundation—one block on another, reinforced steel rods of guilt, and layers of self-condemning plaster—in efforts to hide ourselves. Ultimately we create an edifice that seals others out while destroying ourselves. A prison of despair is often the result. However elaborate our cover-ups, it's impossible to seal out the drive to atone for wrongs in some way or another. We are finally imprisoned in self-condemnation. Self-condemnation always leads us on a search for self-atonement—a path *away from* the Cross.

In his book *Search for Identity,* Earl Jabay describes the process of self-destructive atonement devised by people struggling with guilt:

> This is clearly seen in mental illness, *but all of us use it in varying degrees.* Actually, we would do better to speak of such illnesses as being in the area of our emotions or feelings rather than in the mind itself. Illness on the level of emotionality manifests itself by such things as agonizing anxiety, overpowering fears, destructive rage, repetitive acts which we find difficult to control, the cessation of rational thoughts and speech, suicidal tendencies, fighting bizarre thoughts. These are some of the major ways in which the feelings become ill. Notice that in every symptom mentioned here, the purpose seems to be to say or do something to break down or even destroy the person.
>
> What is that destructive force in the person? I agree with O. Hobart Mowrer *(The Crisis in Religion and Psychiatry)* that the great destroyer in people is their guilt. All people have built and are struggling for ways to dispose of it, one of which is through mental illness.[6]

If unresolved guilt is that serious an issue—and the Tempter knows it is—then it is important for us to know how to deal with it. We must face it, understand it, and discover what God has done for us to resolve the matter. Guilt may cause a person to confuse neediness with worthlessness. To assume that we are hopelessly without worth is to reinforce our vulnerability to temptation and despair.

Feelings vs. Facts

There is an important difference between guilt feelings and real guilt that we must never ignore. From all appearances, some people never get the message no matter how often they hear it. False guilt can have the same destructive impact on us as real guilt. How do we begin to understand the difference? By following Jesus' example and facing the issue head-on. Jesus' consistent approach toward those who came to him was to take their guilt into account. Characteristically he said, "Your sins have been forgiven you." Far from minimizing sins, Christ often raised the issue of sin with those who themselves failed to do so. He addressed sin and guilt openly.

Guilt before God has little to do with guilt feelings. Feelings can be deceptive, and they may not always turn on facts. Satan tempts us to assume that feelings are always true. On one hand, we may feel guilty and think God has something against us when that is not the case. On the other hand, we may not feel any guilt when, in fact, we are guilty before God. John White grapples with this problem in his book *The Fight*.

> Guilt is both a legal status and a feeling which results when law has been violated. . . . But how shall we describe the feeling of guilt? I believe its basic ingredient is an anxious anger directed against oneself. This is why guilt is such an uncomfortable feeling. . . . The irreligious contend that guilt is not a status before law but merely a feeling, and one, moreover, which is best ignored. I must admit that the irreligious man is logically consistent. If God and His law are ignored, it follows that the state and feeling of guilt are ignorable.

> My point here is that our guilt is real. We have it because we have sinned. Our sins—the evil words spoken, our murderous hatreds, our adultery either in the heart or in act, our deceptions, our countless idolatries—all rise up against us to bedevil us with guilt, of whose reality we are only too keenly aware, if we believe.[7]

Denying sin only increases guilt and intensifies its effects on us. The really unforgivable sin is the denial of sin, because by its nature there is then nothing to be forgiven. If we believe we do not sin, we have only to ask our wives, our children, our employers, or our employees. They will set us straight. Bishop Sheen once stated,

> There has been no single influence which has done more to prevent man from finding God and rebuilding his character, has done more to lower the moral tone of society than the denial of personal guilt. . . . The excuses are new—the effort to escape responsibility for our ills is ancient. Through the ages man has always tried to find something to blame besides himself, e.g. poverty, environment, systems of economics, politics, finances, or society in general. . . . Recently, the materialists hit upon a new scapegoat—not in nature, nor society, but inside of man himself, namely, his unconscious. The fault was now, not in the stars, but in that part of ourselves which could not be held responsible."[8]

People who know they have guilt and face it are not so prone to gossip about the weaknesses of others, because they are only too conscious of their own weaknesses.

False Accusations

Satan may also try to enslave us, however, by tempting us to accept guilt without accepting God's grace. It is important to remember that Satan has no power to accuse us with true guilt, because guilt has been taken care of by Jesus Christ. Yet false accusation remains one of Satan's favorite weapons.

The weapon Satan uses often is our feelings. Unfortunately, many Christians equate spirituality with good feelings and happiness; they assume conversely that the lack of good feelings indicates spiritual failure. In doing so, they allow Satan to plant a minefield, where any given step may cause explosions of shrapnel that can maim even the most sincere believer with discouragement and self-condemnation and perhaps depression.

The other side of the picture, however, is that nonbelievers tend to write off guilt as only guilt feelings. As believers we are aware that Satan can use our feelings to delude us into inadequacy and self-condemnation. We may ask why as believers we allow false guilt to hurt us. We may ask how we deal with guilt feelings. How do we overcome their effects?

John addresses these questions in the Book of Revelation.* In regard to the Last Judgment, John writes,

> Now have come the salvation and the power and the kingdom of our God, and the authority of his Christ. For the *accuser* of our brothers, who *accuses* them before our God day and night, has been hurled down (Revelation 12:10, italics mine).

John states that the work of the Evil One is not to kill us, but disable us. Satan tempts us with feelings of guilt that make us think we have real guilt.

In reading various accounts of World War II battles, I discovered that the Nazis developed a strategy to only wound the enemy, not to kill him. Why? The wounding of one soldier forced others to leave the battle to come to the rescue. By wounding soldiers the Nazis could cause others to become nonfunctional as well.

When we yield to Satan's temptation of false guilt, we cannot serve freely in the Lord's army. We withdraw

*Perhaps you feel, as I did for a long time, that Revelation is a mysterious book that is impossible to understand. For years I was put off by complicated charts covered with bizarre pictures and symbols. But there is no need to be afraid of the book. The same rules that govern the study of other books in the Bible govern Revelation. The same principles of interpretation apply.

from the battle and begin a journey inward toward despair and self-condemnation.

We are vulnerable to this temptation at any time, day or night. Satan can accuse us falsely at the times when we least expect it. John White comments,

> Where does he accuse? He accuses you "before our God." When you kneel to pray, his accusations will echo through the vault of your skull. When you seek to bear witness of Jesus, he will scream to God of your vile unworthiness; and if you ever try to preach in public—watch out! He will rant and rave before God in your hearing about the foulness of the lips that attempt to preach God's Word.[9]

Perhaps you wonder how we can possibly distinguish between true guilt and erroneous feelings of guilt. Scripture tells us that "when he [the Holy Spirit] comes, he will convict the world of guilt in regard to sin. . . ." (John 16:8). If this is true, how do we discern the difference between false guilt inflicted by the Accuser and true guilt addressed by the Holy Spirit?

The Holy Spirit Restores

What is the Tempter trying to do, and what is the Holy Spirit trying to do? The Holy Spirit seeks to restore the primary relationship that has been damaged because of sin. The moment we acknowledge that we are sinners, we accept the work of the Holy Spirit. The Spirit works in our lives to restore our relationship with God. When we acknowledge our sin we are free.

The enemy, on the other hand, seeks to drive a wedge between us and God. He can then victimize us with guilt that leads only to more guilt and still more guilt. When we confess our sins but begin to question our sincerity with an increased feeling of guilt, that is the Accuser's work. Whenever you sin, whose help do you need most? God's! If you think God has something against you, you will turn away when you need his love. If you still feel guilty after you have acknowledged your sin and remembered that you are forgiven, it is not God who is accusing you. You need to see this as a temptation from the Tempter.

A Search for Sincerity

When Christians confuse true guilt and false guilt, they may lead nonbelievers into wrong perceptions of the Christian faith. John White says,

> When psychoanalysts raise the question of false (neurotic) guilt, they are raising a perfectly biblical point. We may disagree with them as to the *content* of false guilt (that is, what should make you feel guilty and what shouldn't), but about the existence of the phenomenon they are right on the ball.[10]

What a secular psychoanalyst sees in many Christians is not only unhealthy but unnecessary. How does it feel to be a victim of the Accuser? We confess our sins, and though we are forgiven, Satan tempts us to think we have not been totally sincere. "Perhaps I need to cry a little more and generate a little more guilt." "Maybe a public confession would help." The result? Confusion and a feeling of worthlessness. Perhaps we try talking to our pastor, priest, or rector to help. Afterward, like a scratched record repeating the same note over and over again, Satan says, "You just were not quite sincere enough. Now you need to pray a little more to become more sincere." This syndrome drives us inward, resulting in despair and self-hate. If pressures come, we may pretend they don't exist—while inside, Satan's accusations eat away at our sense of worth before God and others.

More confession usually follows. We confess the temptation, besetting sin, sinful attitude—and in response the Accuser says, "You will do it again, so what's the use? Maybe you ought to go into full-time Christian work to mitigate your guilt. Then you will be spiritual."

The writer of Hebrews calls this process "dead works." Consider these two passages that make a similar point:

> For it is by grace you have been saved, through faith—and this not from yourselves, it is the gift of God—not by works so that no one can boast. For we are God's workmanship, created in Christ Jesus to do good works, which God prepared in advance for us to do (Ephesians 2:8–10).

> How much more shall the blood of Christ, who through the eternal Spirit offered himself without spot to God, purge your conscience from dead works to serve a living God? (Hebrews 9:14 KJV).

Both writers state that works of service are to be part of the experience of Christ's followers. However, the writer of Hebrews tell us that the work of Christ cleanses our consciences from another kind of work—the work we do with the motive of trying to prove ourselves spiritually or to buy off God's forgiveness. In both passages, grace is the central theme. Grace is a gift that enables us to be freed from neurotic guilt and neurotic behavior manifesting itself in dead works.

Grace Is Essential

The apostle Paul tells the church in Rome that understanding grace is essential to overcoming temptation and sin. "For sin shall not be your master, because you are not under law, but under grace" (Romans 6:14).

We learn from Scripture that we need to understand grace if we are to be free from neurotic guilt. But there is room for more confusion here if we aren't careful. It is law that teaches us to distinguish between right and wrong, good works and bad. Yet Paul says we are under grace, not under law.

> At first glance this looks confusing. But notice that the word *law* is not preceded by the article *the*. Whenever such an article is missing, the noun *law* speaks of a principle. Paul is saying that God accepts us, not because we keep the Law, but by and because of grace. However, He is not abolishing the absolutes of the Law itself.[11]

The law is the guideline for our good works. When we view law instead of grace as the means of acceptance by God, we put ourselves under the pressure of fear and rejection. The Accuser can tyrannize us endlessly: "You missed Bible study." "You hypocrite, look at you—going to teach Sunday school and fighting in the car all the way!" And we get more angry because we have lost our temper. We get more depressed because we have normal feelings of discouragement. No wonder the various schools on analytical psychology consider many Christians neurotic.

When we stand before the judgment seat of Christ and God asks us, "By what merits do you enter my kingdom?" what will be our response? "I died to sin"? "I enter on the merits of my deep spirituality"? "I practiced the presence of God"? These are all inadequate. God never accepts us on the basis of our spirituality. God only accepts us on the merits of Christ's work. The only adequate response will be, "I had faith in Christ." This is what grace is all about. Grace, God's gift, frees us from false measurements so that we can be healthy. This freedom allows us to serve God with works that are good because they flow from forgiven and thankful hearts. Dead works are forced—the results of the Tempter's attacks.

Our Call as a Church

Our call in the church is not to advertise our perfection, but to admit our need for God's grace. That recognition frees us to be responsible adults, face temptation, resist the Accuser, and make constructive changes in our lives.

Dietrich Bonhoeffer states it well.

> The Church is precisely that community of human beings which has been led by the grace of Christ to the recognition of guilt towards Christ. To say, therefore, that the Church is the place of the recognition of guilt is nothing but a tautology. If it were otherwise, she would no longer be the Church. The Church today is that community of men which is gripped by the power of the grace of Christ so that, recognizing as guilt towards Jesus Christ both its own personal sin and the apostasy of the western world from Jesus Christ, it confesses this guilt and accepts the burden of it. It is in her that Jesus realizes His form in the midst of the world. That is why the Church alone can be the place of personal and collective rebirth and renewal.[12]

God calls us to deal with real guilt, not just guilt feelings. Real guilt can be dealt with only through the grace of Christ. How do believers overcome this Evil One who tempts us with darts poisoned with guilt? The apostle John answers,

> They overcame him by the blood of the Lamb and by the word of their testimony; they did not love their lives so much as to shrink from death (Revelation 12:11).

Overcoming Is Found Only in Christ

When I was living in Switzerland, I remember attending a little church where I was annoyed by some exposed beams above the chancel. These beams were obviously old and made the church look as if it had not been finished for several hundred years. After the service I asked the pastor why these beams were protruding from the walls and ceiling. He was more than willing to clarify the issue for me.

Before the Reformation, the pastor said, people felt that only the spiritually mature, the clergy (those in full-time Christian work), could worship. These leaders worshiped behind a carved grillwork that separated them from the people. The congregation came to observe the full-time Christian workers at worship behind the grillwork. Of course, the congregation would never consider going behind the separation—they were never spiritual enough. During the Reformation, the grillwork was ripped out, but the beams were left as a reminder to following generations that all believers have access to God directly.

Jesus rent the veil in the temple at his death to provide free access to all. If you have accepted Christ as Savior, you are in full-time Christian work—whether that be the ministry of motherhood, teaching, pastoring, business, or fashion modeling. There are no grillworks or veils with Christ. Spiritual hierarchies do not exist in God's kingdom. We all have equal standing at the foot of the cross. We all overcome our guilt and fears of rejection by God through the blood of the Lamb.

The grillworks of the twentieth century may not be carved out of wood, but they exist nevertheless. "If you will follow my formula, then you will have health and wealth—you can indulge in materialism to your heart's content." "Follow me, your spiritual shepherd, and I will give you all the answers." The religious elite of the present may wear three-piece suits rather than black robes. They may hide behind the electronic grillwork of television, or behind the glossy grillwork of a Christian "best-seller" paperback. But the call remains the same: "Follow us—measure your lives by our spirituality."

Christ has freed us by his death and resurrection to come before God with confidence. Not only the "spiritual elite" may worship; Christ has ripped out the grillwork and we are all free to face God.

Overcoming Through a Clear Witness

We overcome the accusations of Satan by "the word of testimony." We dismantle the minefields of false guilt by giving witness to the work of Christ in history. God did the work for us. Acceptance is not based on our feelings of spirituality, or lack of them. Scripture assures us that we are accepted by almighty God. Neither the Tempter, nor any other accusers either within the church or without, threatens that acceptance. This fact is central to resisting the Tempter's accusations.

The writer of Hebrews says, "Let us then approach the throne of grace with confidence, so that we may receive mercy and find grace to help us in our time of need" (4:16).

Overcoming Through Obedience

Finally, we overcome the Tempter's attacks because we are willing to risk death in our obedience to Jesus Christ. Unfortunately, many of us understand Christ's work for us only in regard to our birth into the community of faith. But our call is to live out faith. Faith is *faithfulness.* "The just shall live by faith" (Galatians 3:11 KJV). Who are the just? Those who have responded in faith to the call of God and have been accepted by Christ. This is the Christian. Satan has always tempted believers to live by another way than grace.

The misunderstanding of grace is not a problem unique to our generation, nor was it to the church at the time of the Reformation. It was the primary problem of almost every church in the first century. The Galatians allowed Satan to use false guilt to drive them to legalism; circumcision was their way of proving their acceptance. The Colossians were tempted to follow asceticism; they mistakenly believed that the mysterious insights that followed proved their spirituality. The Corinthians opted for experiences as signs of spirituality.

Others Shape Our Self-Concepts

Paul taught the believers in the first century that because of Christ, they could change their perspectives about themselves. Psychologists today recognize the importance of the way we view ourselves. It is basic to what happens in our lives. They also agree that our view of ourselves is shaped largely by authority figures in our lives and what they think about us. Where did we ever get the idea that we are beautiful or handsome or talented or homely? We were not born with that data. Most of it was fed to us by others—people who may have said, "Isn't she beautiful!"—and you believed them. Do you remember when someone important laughed at you or teased you? Those hurts can be deeply imbedded in the archives of our minds and emotions. Many people carry into adulthood the pain inflicted during their childhood by a parent, priest, pastor, teacher, or Satan himself who saw them as hopelessly weak—and they believed it.

Studies have shown that even intelligence can be affected by the opinions of others. When I studied for a graduate degree at the University of Santa Clara in California and at the Jungian Institute in Switzerland, I was fascinated to explore the Pygmalion Studies. In these experiments, students of inferior intelligence were taken out of their classes and placed with new teachers. The teachers were told that these students had great potential, were late bloomers, and were extremely gifted. These teachers believed what they were told and treated these children accordingly. Soon the students were improving. They began to excel both socially and intellectually.

We are all affected by the way authority figures view us. Tell a young child that he is a hopeless case, and the results will be devastating. The more prestigious the person who defines the label, the more lasting the effects.

Paul writes to help believers face two of the most destructive emotions known to humankind: the fear of rejection, and guilt. It is no coincidence that these are the two emotions Satan continually uses to tempt us. Paul writes,

> When you were dead in your sins and in the uncircumcision of your sinful nature, God made you alive with Christ. He forgave us *all* our sins, having canceled the written code, with its regulations, that was against us and stood opposed to us; he took it away, nailing it to the cross. And having disarmed the powers and authorities, he made a public spectacle of them, triumphing over them by the cross (Colossians 2:13–15, italics mine).

Hal Lindsey explains the historical meaning behind Paul's concept of debts.

> This is a powerful word picture. In the day in which this was written, the word translated as "certificate of debt" was widely known. Whenever a person was convicted in a Roman court, a "certificate of debt" or bond would be prepared. The scribe of the court would itemize and write down every crime for which the person had been convicted. This certificate meant that the prisoner owed Caesar a prescribed payment for those crimes. It would then be taken with the prisoner to wherever he would be imprisoned and nailed to the door of his cell.[13]

"Debts" are failures—all the times in our lives when we have failed in thought, word, or deed. Every single one has been written on a certificate and nailed to the cross. When Jesus cried, "It is finished," he spoke the very words that the first-century courts wrote across the certificate when a debt was paid. The Greek word is *tetelestai,* meaning "paid in full" (John 19:30).

Lindsey adds,

> The verb translated "having forgiven" means something which happens at a point of time that doesn't have to be repeated. A final act. In God's mind, how many does all mean?[14]

When Jesus died, how many of your sins were future? The ones you committed up to yesterday? The temptations you experienced only in the past? No. It included all your sins—past, present, and future. God placed them all on Christ.

Paul reminds us that God's love and grace preceded our faith. Faith is a response to God's love. Satan tempts us to reverse the order and slip into the errors of the Colossians, the Galatians, and the Corinthians. But our debts have been paid, not by our works, but by grace that comes to us through faith.

It Is Good to Be Loved by God

It is good news to know we are loved by God. This is a faith that begins with amateurs. God accepts you with your problems so that you can grow and develop, accept yourself, and trust in him. With all your hopes, fears, struggles, and temptations, you are freed. God's sovereign grace clarifies the confusing difference between your unworthiness and a false sense of worthlessness. Unworthy of God's love, we are made by God's love forever worthwhile. We are free to accept ourselves because God accepts us. Satan tempts us to forget that fact.

David Johnson notes the great impact of acceptance on a person. I do not concur with his solution, but he knows the problem:

> Self-acceptance is a high regard for yourself, a lack of cynicism about yourself. A person's mental health depends deeply on the quality of his feelings about himself. . . . Psychologically healthy individuals see themselves as liked, wanted, acceptable to others, capable, and worthy. Carl Rogers considers self-acceptance to be crucial for psychological health and growth. . . . To help others grow and develop. . . . You must help others become more self-accepting. . . . A self-rejecting person is usually unhappy and unable to form and maintain good

> relationships. For example, a self-rejecting person expects to be rejected by others and will tend to reject others; as a result of his rejection, the people with whom he is interacting will reciprocate by rejecting him; the person's original expectations are then confirmed.[15]

Johnson's observations are exactly right and pinpoint the repercussions of self-rejection.

A Forgotten Truth

The apostle Paul offers a different view of the matter, however, in saying that self-acceptance does not begin in ourselves. Rather, it is grounded in the knowledge that God accepts us unconditionally because of Christ.

A single woman in her late twenties came to her pastor in a time of tremendous temptation and trouble. For several years she had been trying to make herself spiritually mature. She had attended every seminar in her church. She had tried various forms of spiritual gymnastics. But she seemed to get no place. The more she read about others, the more guilty and worthless she felt about herself.

In desperation this woman tried an experiment. Taking three-by-five cards, she wrote on each one of them "I Love God." She then placed them on the car dashboard, the dresser, the mirror, and on the window above the kitchen sink. The result? Satan tempted her with discouragement, despair, and guilt feelings. The harder she tried, the higher the walls seemed between herself and her close friends, and between herself and God. Her efforts at spirituality seemed to drive her away from freedom. Satan had tempted her and succeeded in imprisoning her spiritually and emotionally.

After a long discussion, her pastor said, "Go home and take all the cards and turn them over. Then write, 'God loves me!'" Satan's prison bars were immediately broken.

Johnson observes,

> It is only as you discover that you are loved for what you are, not for what you pretend to be or for the masks you hide behind, that you can begin to feel you are actually a person worthy of respect and love.[16]

The Christian finds this kind of acceptance in God. As we accept God's love for us in Christ, we discover in the process that our neighbors have worth. Loving those neighbors is a likely outgrowth of that.

Scripture tells us that the prescription for our guilt is the good news of Jesus Christ. We overcome the Tempter's accusations by trusting Christ. We now stand before a righteous, holy, and just God totally forgiven, completely in the clear. The Christian faith is simply seeing ourselves through the eyes of Someone who loves us.

God does not call us to have great faith in God but faith in a great God.

—Harold Busséll

Surely the Lord is in this place, and I was not aware of it.

—Jacob

8.

Why Do I Keep Falling—Just When I Overcame?

The young man sitting across from me was troubled and confused. He was ready to abandon his faith. For years he had promised God again and again that he wouldn't fail and wouldn't succumb to a personality weakness—but he did. He kept asking, "Why do I keep repeating the same mistakes? Why does temptation keep bugging me—just when I think I have it conquered?"

Have you ever struggled with this problem? Few people who are honest with themselves will claim that they live above this battle. Most of us are inadequately prepared to deal with repeated patterns of failure in our lives. Many of us have the idea that in time we will straighten things out; the battles are only temporary. Charles Durham remarks that this issue cannot be avoided. He says,

> There is a romantic idea that if in life we do our best, God's grace will make up the difference and keep us out of trouble. That just is not true. Our mistakes, our sins, our misconceptions will eventually work their way into our personality, despite the best intentions. God's will and fine purpose will not prevent our suffering the consequences of not having known how to build the right kind of character.[1]

Scripture records many accounts of great leaders who were overwhelmed by awareness of their frailty, weaknesses, shortcomings, inadequacies, temptations, and repeated battles with failure.

Begin by Admitting

The major battle with repeated failure is admitting it is there. The behavior of the various people involved in the Watergate scandal is an interesting example of this. The entire episode started off as a comparatively low-level crime. Surely this simple break-in was not the kind that would topple a nation's administration and ultimately send the president and his advisers away in disgrace.

Watergate happened because the response of the administration to the original crime was denial and a chain of cover-ups. Ultimately the president was seriously involved in the obstruction of justice. The tragedy of Watergate was not the original break-in—the world of politics is surely populated by worse—but in denial heaped on denial. This event is only a reflection of our own generation's inability to teach us to deal with temptation and failure successfully.

Satan knows our individual weaknesses. He will repeat his attacks on us even though we overcome. Failure is a part of life since the Fall. To deny it makes us increasingly vulnerable to the forces of evil that tempt us in various ways to repeat the same sins.

People who become involved in sexual sins are dismayed that they can behave in ways they never imagined they were capable of. Less conspicuous but equally serious failures are inappropriate and impulsive responses to threatening events or persons. I have known businessmen who, under pressure, responded with decisions that were ethically questionable; they became haunted by this same temptation for years. Whatever the case, we need to learn how to confront repeated temptations successfully.

Success is valued in our society. This only complicates matters. It is difficult to admit to repeated failures in an environment that loves the winner. "Losers" are lonely people. Our culture's criteria for "winning," however, are purely arbitrary—and faulty. At many lamentable points, the church is a part of this "culture of success."

Peter Gillquist suggests,

> "The victorious Christian life" gospel is at best only half true. Don't misunderstand: I don't believe for a moment that being in union with Christ in his church is misery. But it's patently not all victory. To gain victory, you must have battles, some of which will end in defeat. And whoever heard of winning battles without casualties? . . .
>
> Countless evangelicals are buying a "victorious life" theology that tends to promise that once a person is filled with the Spirit, problems are eliminated or at least greatly reduced. Some charismatics are currently facing a sort of "name it and claim it" approach, often accompanied by promises of prosperity for all. But when we allow the Book of Acts to speak to this matter of life in the Spirit, we get a far different picture. In addition to the ecstasy of the post-Pentecost miracles, we also find that Peter and John are arrested; Ananias and Sapphira fall over dead; Peter and the apostles are jailed: Stephen is murdered, followed by a massive persecution of the church; Simon the sorcerer causes great trouble; the Jews plot to kill Paul; Herod kills James; Paul is stoned; Paul and Silas are arrested at Philippi; riots start in Ephesus: Paul is mobbed and imprisoned in Jerusalem; and a great storm at sea shipwrecks him at Malta. It is in the midst of these troubles and defeats that the church is called to victory.
>
> Too often our message of "victory in Jesus" is like the half-time highlights on ABC's Monday Night Football. The network replays only the touchdowns and the long gainers. Rarely do we see the plays that lost yardage, the broken patterns, dropped passes, or injuries. In like manner, are not we evangelicals sometimes guilty of reporting primarily our spiritual highs, implying that

they are the norm, and that spiritual lows just don't occur?[2]

Poor Teaching the Cause

Often difficulty in overcoming vulnerabilities is the result of poor teaching. People who avoid facing their weaknesses may become obsessed with pointing out others' repeated failures; or, they willfully live by hiding their own besetting sins to project an image of the "victorious life." However, it will be only a matter of time before the dam breaks. Unfortunately, when that happens, the wave that follows destroys innocent people in its path.

Eric Fife has aptly observed,

> The idea seems to have gotten about that we cannot effectively witness for Christ until we live "a life of victory." "If I could only get the victory over this sin," we say, "then I could really serve the Lord."
>
> But the secret of serving the Lord is less that we live a life of victory than that we live a life of fellowship and renewal.[3]

Renewed for Service

To be renewed for service assumes continual recognition of our repeated battles with temptation. Jay Adams points out,

> Christ's consistent approach toward those who came to him was to take their failures into account. Indeed, much of his battle was to get followers who would be able to recognize and repent of their failure—and not, as in the obvious case of Peter, quit "once and for all." His characteristic phrase was, "Your sins have been forgiven you."[4]

Far from minimizing besetting sins, Jesus often raised the issue with those who failed to raise it to themselves. If Jesus takes repeated failure seriously, shouldn't we?

The worship of the false god "Success" in our society instills in us this fear of failure and the dread of humiliation. For many, doors close; for others, challenges of "winning at any cost" are foolishly embraced. The latter disregards ethics, integrity, reputation, and relationships in order to achieve "success." To those who follow its way, this kind of success breeds ruthlessness and insensitivity.

It is important to realize that repeated battles with a besetting sin are not failure. Furthermore, not all failure is sin. We may receive a *B* instead of an expected *A*, arrive late, or organize things poorly; these may result from difficulties in development. They are no more sinful than the tumbles taken by a child learning to walk.

Sinful failure is any thought, word, or deed (or lack of deed) that we at least partially intend disobediently. Unfortunately, many people experience the same feelings of guilt, frustrations, and worthlessness regardless of their motivations. It is important to examine the cause of feelings of frustration or failure. We cannot presume that God's Word and standards are the same as our own. They are not. God's purposes are radically different from those encouraged by gods of the world. Vernon Grounds contends that

> The Bible praises the weakness which is strength and denounces the strength which is weakness. It praises the poverty which is wealth and denounces the wealth which is poverty. It praises the dying which is living and denounces the living which is dying. No wonder, then, that it praises the failure which is success and denounces the success which is failure. No wonder, either, that in I Corinthians 3:12 Paul warns us that the achievements which the world prizes as gold, silver, and precious stones God may write off as wood, hay, and stubble. No wonder,

moreover, that when the apostle in the eleventh chapter of Hebrews recalls the follies of God's shining successes, the overwhelming majority turn out to be failures as the world judges failure, people in conflict with their societies, people who like Jesus and Stephen and Paul and Peter died as criminals—not exactly the sort of ecclesiastical dignitaries who get invited to a Presidential Prayer Breakfast.[5]

Faulty Measurements

Without exception, defective criteria will induce defective evaluations. Faulty measurements will ensure ultimate frustration, discouragement, self-destruction, and confusion. The Bible clearly states that God's sovereign grace, love, and care are for broken people—even those who battle with repeated besetting sins.

Have you ever said, "I have made a total mess of my life"? Repeated failures make us feel that our very relationship with God is at stake. Most discouraging is the feeling that God cannot possibly redeem us in our particular situation. The mistaken but popular view that God is present only when we overcome will develop into a personal recognition problem.

When we battle with repeated weaknesses, feelings of despair can intensify our confusion. We may feel that God is nowhere to be found. We fail to see God's presence in our situation.

In the Old Testament, Jacob had a recognition problem. His life was plagued by besetting sins. Jacob and his mother, Rebekah, had spiritualized issues in order to deceive his father, Isaac. His brother, Esau, held a grudge and wanted to kill Jacob. Rebekah was depressed, feeling her life wasn't worth living. Jacob was on the run to his uncle's home. In the midst of these crisis situations, God spoke to Jacob through a dream of a ladder that reached to heaven. After the experience Jacob said, "Surely the

Lord is in this place, and I was not aware of it" (Genesis 28:16).

Like many of us who keep fighting the same old battles, Jacob did not expect God to be around in a time that was unsettled, disruptive, and confused. Jacob did not recognize God in his situation that was teeming with failure and sin. He was absorbed with emotions of guilt, failure, and fear. Like us, he assumed that God is not around when people are battling against themselves. Jacob discovered in the midst of his predicament that "God is sovereign." God *was* there—but Jacob was unaware.

Jacob learned that God is approachable and accessible and never leaves us. God did not respond to Jacob's repeated failures by saying, "Man, have you failed again! I've had it with you!" God did not reject Jacob in his time of need. Instead, he made that ordinary rest stop a significant place. God was there, accepting, loving, caring, and confronting.

When people battle besetting sins repeatedly, they may develop recognition problems similar to Jacob's. It is hard to see the significance of situations in which we find ourselves. Yet Jacob turned the raw materials of that place and experience into a place of worship.

> When Jacob awoke from his sleep, he thought, "Surely the Lord is in this place, and I was not aware of it." He was afraid and said, "How awesome is this place! This is none other than the house of God; this is the gate of heaven."
>
> Early the next morning Jacob took the stone he had placed under his head and set it up as a pillar and poured oil on top of it. He called that place Bethel, though the city used to be called Luz.
>
> Then Jacob made a vow, saying, "If God will be with me and will watch over me on this journey I am taking and will give me food to eat and clothes to wear so that I return safely to my father's house, then the Lord will be my God and this stone that I have set up as a pillar will be

God's house, and of all that you give me I will give you a tenth" (Genesis 28:16–22).

We need to take the raw materials of our experiences, even the times we fail, and turn them into places of worship. Circumstances of our battles with ourselves can become the stuff out of which God brings transformation. The circumstances for some are repeated struggles with particular sins or habits, or confusion. Like Jacob, we need to have our eyes opened so we can say, "Surely the LORD is in this place, and I was not aware of it." That's the first step for dealing with unhealthy behavior patterns.

We may fail to recognize God's presence, but we also fail sometimes to recognize the whole truth about ourselves. It is easy to think of ourselves as worthless and useless. But in reality this is not the case. Battles with self often cause us to confuse being *unworthy* with being *worthless.* God did not see Jacob as worthless. We need to see ourselves from God's perspective.

Neil Warren has observed some of the effects of unhealthy self-recognition.

> I have become convinced that the way we come to feel about ourselves determines to a great degree the kind of lives we live. For instance, careful empirical research has demonstrated repeatedly that an individual's attitude toward himself radically influences his appraisals of others, so that in a very real sense he can love others only as he learns to love himself. And how a person feels about himself is being increasingly recognized as a vital factor in determining his behavior. A large number of studies have demonstrated that a person will tend to behave in ways which are consistent with his self-conception.
>
> If we had time, we could demonstrate how neurosis and character disorders and various types of addiction and broken homes and the frantic search for meaning all emerge from a sense of not liking oneself very well. Overall, it seems to me, we can say that the adequacy of an individual's self-definition basically determines his

> psychological health. The fact is that we have no better index of personality integration than the self-concept.[6]

Continual battles with our self-recognition, failures, and insecurities are not unique to twentieth-century people. In Scripture these issues were at the core of many great leaders' struggles and difficulties. Very few people judge themselves fairly. Some are too sure of themselves, but others—more sensitive, more adult, and more agreeable—fall into a kind of prejudice against themselves. Speaking as a doctor who has had innumerable opportunities to observe all kinds of self-conferred battles with failure, Paul Tournier says,

> The striking thing is the complete hopelessness of any attempt to bring these people to a more objective view. It is no use pointing out all their good qualities. They look upon it as cruel irony, so clear does it seem to them that we are speaking of the very qualities they lack. . . . Think of the countless people whose valuable talents remain forever hidden, sterilized, because they did not receive the necessary encouragement at the right moment. . . .
>
> How difficult it is to encourage those who lack self-confidence. It requires unfailing perseverance. The steady confidence of the doctor (or any other caring, helping person) is but a reflection of the confidence that God places in each of his children. The former can help the patient to discover the latter. Nothing can be of greater assistance to a person who feels that life is too much for him than the certainty that God is interested in him personally, and in all he does, that God loves him personally and has confidence in him.[7]

That is what God did for Jacob. God affirmed his value and worth. Without that affirmation we soon self-destruct.

Don came to faith in Christ in his middle thirties. He was living with his wife in Arizona. Problems for both marriage partners increased over the years, and the marriage ended in a painful and tragic divorce. Don was left with two small children when his wife moved out. The tragedy was compounded by the inability of his church to help him cope with the situation. To complicate matters further, Don's father, who pastored a large church in another state, asked Don not to visit his church for fear of what people would say.

Don began to assume that the attitudes of his church and his father were the same as God's. This mistaken belief led to several years of tragic failures. Don soon developed serious psychological problems. He subconsciously set himself up for failure. He would do things, such as being obnoxious or rude, to cause people to reject him. Therefore he only proved to himself that his tragic assumptions were true. Eventually, through the help and encouragement of a Christian psychologist, Don was able to see the problem, face it, and rebuild his life. However, his case is found countless times in the journals of pastors and counselors.

God Reminds Us of Our Frailty

The dominant theme in Scripture is divine restoration in the face of human weakness. God redeems people who see themselves as losers, as failures, as worthless and inadequate. The problem of repeated failures was central to the life of Moses.

After deciding to follow God, leaving the household of Pharaoh, Moses was immediately challenged with personal battles—not a life of bliss. So reads the record of most saints.

Moses was forced to face several difficult issues. Striving for justice, he murdered an Egyptian. Afraid, he fled. After many years in exile, a very insecure Moses met God.

Moses learned that God does not forsake or reject his people, even when they fail miserably. God knew precisely where Moses was and brought a significant family into his life. God never abandoned him.

> Now a priest of Midian had seven daughters, and they came to draw water and fill the troughs to water their father's flock. Some shepherds came along and drove them away, but Moses got up and came to their rescue and watered their flock.
>
> When the girls returned to Reuel their father, he asked them, "Why have you returned so early today?"
>
> They answered, "An Egyptian rescued us from the shepherds. He even drew water for us and watered the flock."
>
> "And where is he?" he asked his daughters. "Why did you leave him? Invite him to have something to eat."
>
> Moses agreed to stay with the man, who gave his daughter Zipporah to Moses in marriage (Exodus 2:16–21).

Consider the struggles Moses' mother must have faced. She had invested her life in this young miracle, had seen God deliver him and provide the best training for him and the first thing Moses did after identifying with God's people was commit a murder and run. How embarrassing!

He was not even seen for another forty years. There were no verses to claim, since the Bible hadn't been written yet; no seminars to attend; no telephone hot lines to call; not even a cassette ministry to help! Moses disappeared—for forty years. Chances are his mother never saw the answer to her prayers. She could easily have questioned her investment in this gift of God. She may have faced the feelings which often accompany many parents when their children battle with life: "If I only had enough faith, this wouldn't have happened." Scripture never deals with "what ifs," but with what is and what can be.

God Never Abandons Us

If we are struggling with those same old battles, we need the assurance that God never abandons us. God does not discard us any more than he discarded Moses. God knows exactly where we are.

Moses' decision to follow God was challenged by the rude awakening that life remains a test. Moses failed in his first major battle. However, through a wilderness experience he found healing and learned the value of solitude. The wilderness provided time—with no outside help from, say, a seminar or manual to study—to gain personal perspective, face personal limitations, confront weaknesses, and discover strengths.

In the context of this desert experience Moses gained skills and perspectives that enabled him to lead the Hebrew people through a desert to the land of promise. This was not the end of his struggles, however. The miracle of the burning bush did not keep Moses immune from personal battles. They kept repeating themselves like a scratched record.

> The LORD said, "I have indeed seen the misery of my people in Egypt. I have heard them crying out because of their slave drivers, and I am concerned about their suffering. So I have come down to rescue them from the hand of the Egyptians and to bring them up out of that land into a good and spacious land, a land flowing with milk and honey. . . . So now, go. I am sending you to Pharaoh to bring my people the Israelites out of Egypt."
>
> But Moses said to God, "*Who am I,* that I should go to Pharaoh and bring the Israelites out of Egypt?"
>
> And God said, "I will be with you. And this will be the sign to you that it is I who have sent you: When you have brought the people out of Egypt, you will worship God on this mountain."
>
> Moses said to God, "Suppose I go to the Israelites and say to them, 'The God of your fathers has sent me to you,'

> and they ask me, *'What is his name?'* Then what shall I tell them?"
>
> God said to Moses, "I AM WHO I AM. This is what you are to say to the Israelites: 'I AM has sent me to you.' "
>
> God said to Moses, "Say to the Israelites, 'The Lord, the God of your fathers—the God of Abraham, the God of Isaac and the God of Jacob—has sent me to you.' This is my name forever, the name by which I am to be remembered from generation to generation" (Exodus 3:7–15, italics mine).

Moses came face to face with the fact that God knew his name. As great as this experience was, however, it did not insulate Moses from future battles and temptations. Moses still struggled with feelings of inadequacy, insecurity, and fear.

As soon as God challenged Moses to go meet the need, the same old feelings of inadequacy surfaced. God's plan of redemption begins with people capable of failure, not programs promising success.

Past Failures Disable Us

" 'So now, go. I am sending you.'. . . But . . . 'Who am I?' " (Exodus 3:10–11). Moses' protest was not an attempt to escape responsibility. Rather, he struggled continually against self-deception and feelings of worthlessness or inferiority. He began life as a secure, confident, bold person—bold to the point of murdering an Egyptian.

Following that failure, Moses battled feelings of incompetence. He faced the challenge of self-discovery by asking, "Who am I?" God did not respond by saying, "Moses, do you really want to know? After all, you've been proven a failure. I gave you every privilege and you simply blew it. You ought to be ashamed of yourself." God gave none of these responses. Instead he encouraged Moses and said, "I will be with you." God did not hold the former battles or present failures against Moses.

God promises the presence of the Holy Spirit. Many look for an experience from God to rescue them from never-ending battles with temptation; rather, God promises to go with us into our battles.

I wonder if we find God's promises enough for our journey of faith. Jesus Christ promises unconditionally to go with us.

> Therefore, go and make disciples of all nations, baptizing them in the name of the Father and of the Son and of the Holy Spirit, and teaching them to obey everything I have commanded you. And surely I am with you always, to the very end of the age (Matthew 28:19–20).

Jesus didn't say, "If you walk in the Spirit, I will go with you." He promised to be with us until the end of the age. That promise was unconditional. God goes with us, even when we face repeated battles with self and the Devil. Moses learned that the ultimate responsibility for God's work is God's own.

Focus on God

In an encounter with God, Moses asked, "Who am I?" That question can lead to personal chaos. An altered perspective prompted Moses to ask, "Who are you?" (Exodus 3:11–15).

Repeated crises, changes, and difficulties may devastate us personally. But the central issue for us is to understand and ask who God is. John Calvin emphasized that this issue is foundational: "For, in the first place, no man can survey himself without forthwith turning his thoughts towards the God in whom he lives and moves. . . . the knowledge of God and the knowledge of ourselves are bound together by a mutual tie."

If we don't understand who God is, we will place our sins and failures between God and us.

Place God Between You and Your Problem

When people battle temptations, more often than not they place their struggles between themselves and God. Moses learned that God's grace enabled him to place God between himself and his struggles. In a fallen world, Satan will use our problems, failures, and struggles to tempt us to believe that God is rejecting us.

Moses was still hesitant. God respected Moses' insecurity enough to allow Aaron to be his helper. God instructed Moses to use his rod as a sign of God's presence.

A rod was used by a shepherd as a walking stick—a sort of security blanket. This dead, artless piece of wood became the symbol of God's power when Moses stood before Pharaoh, both at the Red Sea and in battle. What was the difference in this artless piece of wood?

> Then the LORD said to him, "What is that in your hand?"
>
> *"A staff,"* he replied.
>
> The LORD said, "Throw it on the ground." . . .
>
> Now the LORD had said to Moses in Midian, "Go back to Egypt, for all the men who wanted to kill you are dead." So Moses took his wife and sons, put them on a donkey and started back to Egypt. And he took the *staff of God* in his hand (Exodus 4:2–3, 19–20, italics mine).

Notice the change. The only difference was in ownership.

Many of us, like Moses, take past mistakes and our feelings of inadequacy to avoid being involved in ministry to people. God promised Moses that Aaron would speak for him. This was in response to Moses' excuse that he was not a good speaker. Satan tempts us to use feelings of inadequacy as excuses to hide behind. In this way we avoid having to be involved with people. It is here that Satan tempts us to opt for practical atheism.

Like us, Moses tried to shift responsibility and to depreciate himself. God's anger was aroused.

> But Moses said, "O Lord, please send someone else to do it."
>
> Then the LORD's anger burned against Moses and he said, "What about your brother, Aaron the Levite? I know he can speak well. He is already on his way to meet you, and his heart will be glad when he sees you. You shall speak to him and put words in his mouth; I will help both of you speak and will teach you what to do. He will speak to the people for you, and it will be as if he were your mouth and as if you were God to him. But take this staff in your hand so you can perform miraculous signs with it" (Exodus 4:13–17).

Moses responded to God's call, but he continued to face difficulties and temptations. He still faced confusion. He continued to do battle with old personality flaws, insecurities, and struggles.

Our Basic Battle Is With Self

The ultimate battle that we all face is not with God's people or a "Pharaoh" who seeks to control us. It is with ourselves and the patterns of temptation that torment us. Worst of all is the war that rages within ourselves. Under real or imagined attack by others, inadequacies, insecurities, and old temptations will surface as they did in Moses. However, it is important to realize that God is not threatened by our battles; we need to pour out questions and complaints to him. God listened to Moses' complaints and gave him power to operate and instructions that moved him out of his self-pity.

As with Moses, it may take us a lifetime to cope with our patterns of repeated failures. Scars of the past, though forgiven, can and do ignite old patterns of behavior.

The Bible portrays its leaders' glorious triumphs as

well as their temptations and failures. Unfortunately, when it comes to temptation, it seems that we don't learn from past mistakes. It is one thing to make a bad investment—we can learn how to be wiser in our stewardship of money; but it's another thing to say we won't yield to a specific temptation again when the same kind of situation presents itself. There is a danger that repeated patterns of behavior can eventually cause psychological dependency to affirm our place in life. It is important to get professional help if and when it is needed.

Look for Patterns

We do well to examine our past failures and struggles with temptation to see if there is a common pattern to our behavior. What led to the failure? What happened afterward? Did we prove to ourselves that we are failures?

Increased knowledge of our patterns of behavior can enable us to protect ourselves from patterns of self-rejection and self-deprecation. Satan tempts us to deal with our repeated failures in one of two ways. We shrug them off—"So what's the big deal?"—or we forgive others while hating ourselves. This self-hate is just another way the Tempter persuades us to avoid change. Bishop Sheen writes,

> Many battles may go on until a person dies, but he need never become depressed about the battle. Nobody in the world can say he has nothing to do, for he has something to do as long as he has something to overcome. Life puts everyone to a test. In fact, our inner weakness is a greater test than outer circumstance.[8]

Obstacles Are Opportunities

What we do with our weaknesses such as alcoholism, lust, or dishonesty, or with our sicknesses and trials, is a test of character. All our obstacles are opportunities to allow God to work in our lives. Changed circumstances do not hinder God's work in a life. God works with broken people who are open to receive love, forgiveness, and new beginnings.

Stuart Briscoe writes movingly of personal battles.

> I can vividly remember the first time I was really confronted with my own failure. It was both excruciating and exhilarating. It was excruciating because out of my love for the Lord I wanted to serve Him wholeheartedly: and yet the more I endeavored to serve Him, the more I appeared to fail Him. The more intimately I knew Him, the more intimately I got to know myself. . . . My self-discovery was a disappointment, to put it mildly. But it was exhilarating because I realized that I was discovering what He had known all the time.[9]

A New Freedom

Facing repeated failures and mistakes frees us from self-reliance, from having to hide them so that they eat us away inside. It frees us to deal with them honestly and openly before God and frees us to face the guilt. To deny repeated temptations and failures is to choose spiritual and emotional bondage.

Paul's claim, "I am the chief of all sinners," was also a claim on God's grace.

> What shall we say, then? Shall we go on sinning so that grace may increase? By no means! We died to sin; how can we live in it any longer? Or don't you know that all of us who were baptized into Christ Jesus were baptized into his death? We were therefore buried with him through baptism into death in order that, just as Christ was raised from the dead through the glory of the Father, we too may live a new life (Romans 6:1–4).

We are not free to continue in our old patterns on the ground that grace abounds. God expects us to take the old ways seriously. God expects progress in our lives.

God wants us to learn from past patterns of failures. Paul faced past challenges that haunted his mind.

> Not that I have already obtained all this, or have already been made perfect, but I press on to take hold of that for which Christ Jesus took hold of me. Brothers, I do not consider myself yet to have taken hold of it. But one thing I do: Forgetting what is behind and straining toward what is ahead, I press on toward the goal to win the prize for which God has called me heavenward in Christ Jesus.
>
> All of us who are mature should take such a view of things (Philippians 3:12–15).

Forgetting what lies behind, I press on. Paul, who held the coats of those who stoned Stephen, said, "We must leave behind the past failures." Do you feel your unending battles make you useless to God? That feeling can be a temptation from Satan.

Face the Facts

Temptations and failures are a fact of life. The issue is not, "Do we fail?" Rather, "What can we do, now that we have failed. How can we respond responsibly?" Recognizing these issues is where we begin to build protection against besetting sins and temptations.

Whatever liberates our spirit without giving us self-control is disastrous.

—*Goethe*

True religion shows its influence in every part of our conduct; it is like the sap of a living tree, which penetrates the most distant boughs.

—*William Penn*

9.

The Gift of Self-Control

Do you remember when your mother made a steaming batch of chocolate chip cookies? You smelled them, you saw them, you wanted them. And your mom said, "You can't have any until after supper tonight. Oh, by the way, I will be going to the store for about an hour." And just as she walked out the door, she called back, "Even though I am not here—God sees you. Have a good time!"

The door slams. She leaves. You are all alone. You check the cookies to see if they are all right. Then you look behind the curtains to see if there is an eye of God looking at you. You just can't find God anyplace. You smell the cookies, and you see them looking at you. A few stragglers are hanging over the edge of the plate. You realize that a few of these are mutants. Hangers-on. They're messing up the neat pile. In fact, you would be doing God and Mom a service by wiping them out.

All of a sudden, a flannel-graph picture comes to mind and you remember the stories of Lot's salty wife and stone-cold Ananias. In spite of this, you finally grab a small straggler on the edge, and you discover that nothing happens. You eat, and no lightning strikes. You fluff out the rest, so Mom will never realize what you've done. Mom comes home—and sure enough, she doesn't even notice!

This is where the issue of self-control begins. After all, what does God care about a few stray cookies? You are right—it's no big deal. The problem is that while your action didn't seem to have any notable external consequences, it nonetheless did damage to your will. You succumbed to a major difficulty that has deceived people since the Garden of Eden. You measured values on the basis of a morality that says, "It's all right as long as you don't get caught."

You waited for God to lay a whammie on you, but God didn't. Each decision we make that embraces such thinking further erodes self-control.

The will—our thoughts, feelings, and mind—is the motivating factor in our lives. By our wills we move toward God and Scripture, or away from them. What we call the *will* Scripture names the *heart.* David's heart was *toward* the Lord; Pharaoh's heart was hardened *against* God's way.

The heart, or will, is the seed from which self-control germinates. It is the most important thing in the Christian's life. The body is directed by the will. Attitudes are controlled and compassion is borne by the will.

The reason why illegal drugs are so damnable is that they confuse the will. The primary thing that God desires is our will. Drugs fragment one's perception of reality, confusing the will.

Psychological Problems

We must not overlook the fact that emotional problems are real and can affect the will. Emotional problems can make us vulnerable to the effects of temptation. Charles Durham points out the seriousness of recognizing this fact.

> Christians are not immune to mental disturbance. Their brains work just as do those of non-Christians; their experiences hit them just as hard; and their understandings promote psychological twistings in the same way.
>
> God does not suspend natural law for us. Gravity is gravity, electricity is electricity, a malfunctioning gland is a malfunctioning gland, and a psychological trauma a psychological trauma. A bad family pattern is exactly that, and confused thought patterns are the same whether one is a believer or not.[1]

Causes of psychological and emotional problems vary. If not treated for what they are, they can limit our ability to deal with and overcome temptation. When facing emotional or psychological problems that hinder our ability to obey Christ, we should seek professional help. The church also has a responsibility to encourage people to seek help in that situation.

Our wills are the taproots of our lives. They enable us to receive God's nourishment. Like a tree planted by the living waters, we will bring forth fruit (Psalm 1). When we deny responsibility we replace the will with mechanisms of avoidance. It is easy to say that someone else is wrong and needs self-control when his or her actions are quite visible ones like stealing, lying, or murder. We can exclaim "They are wrong" or "They ought to be arrested." But when it comes to controlling our own inward attitudes, we strike at the taproot. We avoid responsibility and betray the will by exercising loud judgments about the wrongs of others without acknowledging our own.

God calls us to discipline our wills and face ourselves. Why? The will tells us how to act, how to respond, how to perform. The Word of God provides the target, but only our wills can shoot the arrows. There will be no strength to resist temptation without disciplined wills. The will is the center of all motivation, and therefore it is the taproot of character.

Some people have difficulty with temptation simply

because they lack sufficient knowledge of what God expects. Never having disciplined their minds to the teachings of Scripture, they are markers on the path. Other people overreact and become discouraged when they find that all their battles with temptation are not won immediately. Others may fail to develop their wills because they have hidden fears of failure. In any case, the Word of God assumes that our wills can and must be trained.

Attitudes, not actions, are God's primary concern. Actions flow from attitudes. God is concerned about what is happening inside a person. That is where self-control begins.

In this age of anesthesia we seldom see the effects of suffering. We would be in a sad state, however, if there were no pain. To a doctor, pain is an external sign of internal strife. People rarely die of pain; pain is merely the body's cry for help.

On a mission trip to the Dominican Republic, my daughter and I visited a leper colony. The community was ministered to daily by an order of Roman Catholic nuns. The sister in charge informed us that the tragedy of leprosy is that its victim feels no pain. A person may develop a sore on his or her foot and not know it. There are no headaches or upset stomachs, just internal deterioration. How appropriate that the Bible should use leprosy as a symbol of sin. The last thing we want to do, but the first we need to do, is cry "Help!"

Hurts May Be Good

Hurts let you know something is wrong. Our generation seems to operate on the principle that if nothing hurts, then nothing is wrong. We develop a scale of sins, from bad to worst. Worst are the sins which *show the most*—for instance, a woman caught in adultery. But Jesus reminds us that if there is a "worse," it lies in the less external matter of attitude, of what the accusers have wrong beneath their religious robes. Leprosy of the will is easily disguised, especially from the self, until it's too late for help.

Excuses will not do. The apostle Paul said that God will provide a way out of each situation and we will be held accountable for how we respond.

> So, if you think you are standing firm, be careful that you don't fall! No temptation has seized you except what is common to man. And God is faithful; he will not let you be tempted beyond what you can bear. But when you are tempted, he will also provide a way out so that you can stand up under it (1 Corinthians 10:12–13).

We need to begin, in this matter of self-control, with the unseen internal issues of the will that each of us faces daily. God's concern with the child and the cookies was with the heart—the will—not with the game-playing attitude or with the cookie-snatching itself.

We are never left alone. When Mom walks out of the door God really does stay—not as an ogre to prevent pleasure, but to help and provide a way out. Embedded in Paul's statement "God has provided a way out . . ." is the truth "God is there." We are bombarded by a constant stream of destructive stimuli. They all encourage us to believe the myths that "If I don't get caught, no one is really hurt." Added to this are our own desires that tell us that cookies taste good. These messages say, "Taste and see." They come from the world of Madison Avenue. They are values taught on the television screen, movies, and radio. Soap operas, slick magazine ads, and the fads of each decade tempt us to avoid the conflicts of the will, to enjoy, to give in, to eat the cookies.

In a letter to first-century believers, James instructs Christians that both tests and temptations are unavoidable in this life. The tests or trials of life can make us vulnerable to the Tempter's traps, especially when we are tired or feel we cannot face one more problem and feel we are caught by life itself.

James tries to help these believers see first that tests are normal and God has a purpose in them. We must be careful, however, not to confuse trials with temptations.

> Consider it pure joy, my brothers, whenever you face trials of many kinds, because you know that the testing of your faith develops perseverance. Perseverance must finish its work so that you may be mature and complete, not lacking anything. If any of you lacks wisdom, he should ask God, who gives generously to all without finding fault, and it will be given to him. But when he asks, he must believe and not doubt, because he who doubts is like a wave of the sea, blown and tossed by the wind. That man should not think he will receive anything from the Lord; he is a double-minded man, unstable in all he does (James 1:2–8).

"*Whenever* you face trials," not *if* you face them. Tests are unavoidable. However, there is a purpose for them: they teach us endurance. James assures us that God will provide stability, which is essential for facing temptation. Certainly we get tired of hassling issues at the office or in the home, yet God wants our taproots to grow in the soil provided for us. God's redemptive power is at work in our difficulties.

James calls us to be realists when it comes to tests and trials. Why? So we will be realists when it comes to facing temptation. James writes,

> When tempted, no one should say, "God is tempting me." For God cannot be tempted by evil, nor does he tempt anyone; but each one is tempted when, by his own evil desire, he is dragged away and enticed. Then, after desire has conceived, it gives birth to sin; and sin, when it is full-grown, gives birth to death.
>
> Don't be deceived, my dear brothers. Every good and perfect gift is from above, coming down from the Father of the heavenly lights, who does not change like shifting shadows. He chose to give us birth through the word of truth, that we might be a kind of firstfruits of all he created (James 1:13–18).

This passage distinguishes between temptation to evil and testing, which was addressed earlier in the epistle. James contrasts the excuses a person being tempted may make with the facts of the case. We might wonder about this language, which seems to contradict the words of Paul in 1 Corinthians 10:13 and the words of Jesus in the Lord's Prayer.

Two Kinds of Temptation

The temptations that Paul and Jesus speak of come from without, whereas James refers to temptation from within. The kind James has in mind arises from uncontrolled passions and appetites. Our weakness in yielding to these sins cannot be excused by casting the responsibility on God. The real source of temptation is found within us. James says each person is tempted by his or her own lust. James then reaffirms God's faithfulness: "God does not change." He is holy. So James continues to say that the will must be subject to self-control.

> My dear brothers, take note of this: Everyone should be quick to listen, slow to speak and slow to become angry, for man's anger does not bring about the righteous life that God desires. Therefore, get rid of all moral filth and the evil that is to prevalent, and humbly accept the word planted in you, which can save you.
>
> Do not merely listen to the word, and so deceive yourselves. Do what it says. Anyone who listens to the word but does not do what it says is like a man who looks at his face in a mirror and, after looking at himself, goes away and immediately forgets what he looks like. But the man who looks intently into the perfect law that gives freedom, and continues to do this, not forgetting what he has heard, but doing it—he will be blessed in what he does.
>
> If anyone considers himself religious and yet does not keep a tight rein on his tongue, he deceives himself and his religion is worthless. Religion that God our Father

accepts as pure and faultless is this: to look after orphans and widows in their distress and to keep oneself from being polluted by the world (James 1:19–27).

This is a call to action. It is a call to take the will and choose to be other-oriented. James tells us that those who listen but do not use their will to respond are like those who look into a mirror and walk away. A mirror gives a deceptive picture of reality. It shows us the facts, but everything is reversed. Without a response from the will, our view of life will be like a picture in a mirror. It will lead to deception and faulty self-perception.

Trials and temptations are normal in life. We need not feel guilty about having them. It is easy to feel guilty about the wrong things. We may feel guilty about the struggle but not about the act. God's Word seeks to correct our perception. We must not feel guilty because we struggle. Temptations are tests that are a part of life. They provide opportunities to grow, develop, and discover God's faithfulness and grace.

But what then did Jesus mean when he said, "Lead us not into temptation, but deliver us from evil"? Isn't this a contradiction?

These words in the context of the Lord's Prayer are similar to what James explains. This petition is often wrongly divided, but both the context and the Greek language reveal there is unity between the clauses. The adversative particle *but* placed in the middle binds these two ideas together. William Barclay suggests that the sentence means, "In order that we may not be led into temptation, deliver us from evil."[2] Christ asks us to pray that out of the consciousness of our own weaknesses, we ask God to defend us by protecting us.

John Stott makes the point that the "evil should be rendered the evil one. In other words, it is the devil who is in view, who tempts God's people to sin, and from whom we need to be protected. So behind these words that Jesus gave us to pray are the implications that the devil is too strong for us, that we are too weak to stand up to him, but that our heavenly Father will deliver us if we call on him."[3]

A Forgotten Gift

During recent decades much emphasis has been placed on the gifts of the Spirit. Seminars, sermons, and lectures have focused on the gift of tongues, the gift of evangelism, and the gift of teaching. But the gift of self-control has received much less attention. The apostle Paul writes to the first-century Christians on the subject.

> But the fruit of the Spirit is love, joy, peace, patience, kindness, goodness, faithfulness, gentleness and self-control (Galatians 5:22-23).

As one of the fruit of the Holy Spirit, self-control is to be an expected result of conscientious Christian living. But it is not the fruit of the Spirit that will evoke applause from our friends. Moreover, few people are delighted by challenges to be more disciplined. "I would rather have something more spiritual." "Obedience and self-control just aren't devotional enough." "Perhaps something a little more evangelistic might do." "Self-control sounds like another one of those salvation-by-works schemes." "Obedience is just another strait jacket to keep me from living life to its fullest."

Church history has been marked by communities that have found the world's arena too threatening and unmanageable. In reaction, they have sought to shrink back from the crowd. In the name of obedience, Christians have sought to amputate limbs of humanity that have proven difficult to control. Vows of poverty have been taken to avoid materialism. Renunciation has become a way of life for many. We must remember, however, that it can also be very self-centered.

Renunciation is neither obedience nor self-control. Rather, it is an amputation of the will. A key phrase used in Scripture is "yielding to God." We must not think of "yield" as a passive word. It means choosing, using our wills, igniting self-control to follow God. Notice the active nature of self-control and Christian character in this statement by Paul:

> Love must be sincere. Hate what is evil; cling to what is good. Be devoted to one another in brotherly love. Honor one another above yourselves. Never be lacking in zeal, but keep your spiritual fervor, serving the Lord. Be joyful in hope, patient in affliction, faithful in prayer. Share with God's people who are in need. Practice hospitality (Romans 12:9–13).

The work of yielding to the Holy Spirit's activity in our lives consists primarily of choosing to obey God's direction for our lives. Without the work of God's Spirit within, our efforts will be frustrated. We have been given grace to free us to serve God. "Yielding" means choosing to allow Christ to be Lord, day by day, hour by hour.

How much simpler it would be if one experience of the power of the Holy Spirit in our lives could flood us for all time with the glory of God. It did not happen to the first-century Christians (otherwise we would not have New Testament writings after Acts 4). Spiritual experiences are just as real for us as they were for the early church. However, the early church still had to be instructed to choose holiness as a lifestyle. God will never take the power of choice away from the believer—it is a gift. It is that gift for which we will stand accountable before God.

Trust and Work

In light of this truth we do two things. First, we find our security in the promise that Christ will never leave us nor forsake us. Second, we do exactly what Peter told believers to do—*after* the spiritual high of Pentecost had dissipated.

> For this very reason, make every effort to add to your faith goodness; and to goodness, knowledge; and to knowledge, self-control; and to self-control, perseverance; and to perseverance, godliness; and to godliness, brotherly kindness; and to brotherly kindness, love. For if you possess these qualities in increasing measure, they will keep you from being ineffective and unproductive in your knowledge of our Lord Jesus Christ (2 Peter 1:5–8).

In our permissive society the call to control comes in every shape, size, and model: control unruly hair, control body odor, management control, temperature control. Yet we have few controls for conflicts that erupt from within ourselves. In the United States alone, a violent crime is committed every twenty seconds. Someone is murdered every twenty-three minutes. Obviously, more is needed than the images and promises of control handed out to us.

The gift of self-control is basic to our development and is a primary resource that enables us to manage our lives. It is foundational for developing any talent, temperance, or discipline and for warding off attacks by the Evil One.

Self-control assumes that we know ourselves, our weaknesses, our destructive patterns of behavior, and our vulnerabilities. Self-control is the shaping factor in our lives. People do not lose their faith; they fail to shape their lives by it. Self-control is the thing that forms our behavior, because every impression is a preparation for an expression. By our wills we engage self-control.

> For though we live in the world, we do not wage war as the world does. The weapons we fight with are not the weapons of the world. On the contrary, they have divine power to demolish strongholds. We demolish arguments and every pretension that sets itself up against the knowledge of God, and we take captive every thought to make it obedient to Christ (2 Corinthians 10:3–5).

If we fail to understand God's goal for our lives, our vulnerabilities will ruin us emotionally and spiritually.

Practical Guidelines

SEE YOURSELF THROUGH GOD'S EYES

J. B. Phillips paraphrases Paul's words to the church in Rome this way: "Don't cherish exaggerated ideas of yourself or your importance, but try to have a sane estimate of your capabilities by the light of the faith that God has given to you all" (Romans 12:3).

It is important for us to see ourselves as God sees us. Do our perceptions square with reality? We need to examine ourselves carefully and humbly, for we are stewards of truth and must submit ourselves to the truth that we see. We are not free to innovate or rearrange reality; nor are we to alter the terms of God's vision for our lives. To begin with, we do not need to apologize for our personal experiences. It is in the context of these that we gain self-control.

UNDERSTAND STEWARDSHIP

Individualism and self-centeredness result in a loss of control, of vitality, of life. Ironically, when the Tempter whispers, we respond, "I must live my own life." Or, "It is my own body, and I can do with it what I want."

A young woman considering an abortion kept repeating, "It's my body, and I can do with it what I want." I asked her if it really was her own body. Could she keep it out of the grave, or keep it from wrinkling? All gifts from God are but gifts on loan.

We will never have resources for self-control if we believe that our bodies and lives are exclusively our own. Have you ever noticed how much better you treat borrowed things than your own? Remember how much more carefully you guarded your friend's tennis racquet, guarding it so that there would be no scratches. Why? Because it belonged to someone else . . . you'd better take care of it!

All gifts have been given to us, by God, on loan. Each

gift will eventually be taken away. Our minds will go at some point, limbs and bodies will fail, material possessions will be divided among others or end up in probate court. We are stewards of these things, not owners. We have been purchased by Christ at a great price. These valuable—yes, priceless—selves are now ours to steward.

> Flee from sexual immorality. All other sins a man commits are outside his body, but he who sins sexually sins against his own body. Do you not know that your body is a temple of the Holy Spirit, who is in you, whom you have received from God? You are not your own; you were bought at a price. Therefore honor God with your body (1 Corinthians 6:18–20).

KNOW YOUR WEAKNESSES

The best way to build self-control is to have a realistic understanding of personal strengths and weaknesses. Weakness should not be confused with sin, or with loss of favor with God or others. Everyone has peculiar weaknesses or vulnerabilities. And they can cause us to sin.

Write down in two columns your weaknesses and your strengths. Leave enough room under each entry to list the positive and negative effects of each item. Strengths can have negative outworkings, just as weaknesses can produce positive results.

Jim is a gregarious person and liked by almost everyone. This is a gift. The positive outworking of this is that Jim is able to relate to a wide variety of people and build relationships. The negative outworking of it is that Satan tempts him to manipulate others when he is being confronted. It is important for Jim to see both the negative and positive effects of all his strengths and weaknesses. Self-control needs to be exercised over both weaknesses and strengths.

The apostle Paul's thorn in the flesh was the very

thing that made him dependent on God's strength. It was what made Paul strong (see 2 Corinthians 12:7–10).

Now take more paper and trace your behavior patterns. Write them out and examine what occurred before the weakness surfaced. For example, Mary, a married woman, noticed that in her life there would be times when she would struggle with fantasies of running away—perhaps with another man. After tracing the patterns, she noticed that she was most vulnerable to these fantasies when other people, and especially her own family, were placing controls over her life. What she eventually realized was that her fantasies of romantic getaway gave her a sense of the control she felt deprived of. The basic problem was not sexual in any significant way. Once she was able to see this she was able to address the appropriate problem.

It is important to understand and to face both the pattern and the weakness. If we have a problem with alcohol, we should not work in a bar or build a wine cellar. If we are tempted to steal, we shouldn't count the Sunday morning offerings after church. We must stand against the problems.

In counseling others I have found that the weaknesses of most people seem to follow a pattern. A close examination will help us to break a pattern of behavior roller-coasting toward disaster. Sometimes we need help, such as counseling, to discover those patterns of behavior. It is a strength, not a weakness, to ask for counseling; it indicates that we are strong enough to ask for help. "Weak" persons hate to appear helpless.

Some patterns of behavior become so ingrained that we may need to get professional help. Many pastors, counselors, and psychologists are trained to deal with specific weaknesses and neurotic patterns of behavior. Problems can provide a sense of security to some people. Therefore it is important to deal with them. Even under the guise of prayer we can pray ourselves into our weaknesses. Our entire lives can become obsessed with a single problem.

Consider, for example, the temptation to lust and sexual sin. We can easily pray, "Lord, help me not to think about sex. Lord, you know how obsessed I get by sex. Lord, help me not to be so obsessed with . . ." Suddenly our minds move from prayer into a sexual fantasy. There is always a risk of becoming so obsessed with besetting sin that we feed it like a lion in a cage. The more problems they are fed, even through prayer, the stronger they get. We may even need short-term professional help at this point to break the pattern.

DON'T FOCUS ON JUST ONE PROBLEM

It is important to examine life to see if we are developing in other aspects of our lives before Christ. Satan tempts us to see ourselves as *problems* rather than *people with problems.* When this happens, we focus so intently on our problems that other important areas of our lives are left undeveloped. We may avoid relationships and resources.

Most of our sinful problems and obsessions are born out of legitimate needs created by God. We should take the time to examine the basic need underlying a problem. Is it a need for God? For relationships? For security? For controls in life? It is important that we not feel guilty about these basic legitimate needs.

God will not help us as long as we continue to live in a realm of fantasy and unreality. Problems need to be named and faced for what they are. If it is bitterness, call it bitterness. If it is lust, don't hide from it or spiritualize it. Self-deception manifests itself partially in rationalizing and spiritualizing. The longer we deceive ourselves in this way, the deeper the problem becomes, cutting away at the taproot of self-control. Unacknowledged problems will not be solved with time. If we need help from a trusting friend, we should get it.

DEMYTHOLOGIZE THE TEMPTATION

The writer of an article in *Leadership* magazine points out the necessity of demythologizing temptations.

> Sexual stimulations promise a lie. Cheryl Tiegs is not going to be with you—in fact, photo sessions that create sexy photos are tiresome and mechanical, not at all erotic. Recognize that *Playboy* centerfolds are touched up in the miracle of dry-transfer printing, that they represent an unrealizable ideal of sexuality that does not include feelings of impotence, awkwardness, monthly menstrual periods, and many other reminders of humanity. Life is far different from what soft porn portrays it to be.[4]

I would stress the importance of doing this same kind of demythologizing with any temptation—temptation to materialism, greed, or any other vice.

Scripture always points to the balance, the tension, between God's work in our lives and our own choices. God expects us to act in faith and to take responsibility for our own actions—to activate the taproot of our own wills. Paul encouraged the Philippians, "Continue to work out your salvation with fear and trembling" (2:12). But he does not lay the matter totally on their shoulders. We need not feel inadequate. Paul adds, "It is God who works in you to will and to act according to his good purpose" (2:13).

There is no easy solution to overcoming temptation. I wish there were. I would market it, package it, print it in a binder, and hold weekly seminars. No. Temptation and trials are always with us. But so is Jesus Christ in the person of the Holy Spirit, who has promised to be with us until the end of the age. Self-control begins by reminding ourselves that the Lord never leaves us or forsakes us. God goes with us and remains with us even when we revel and allow ourselves to wallow in a quagmire of lust and greed. That is God's business.

Writing to a friend, C. S. Lewis addressed this difficult issue of self-control.

> I know all about the despair of overcoming chronic temptations. It is not serious, provided self-offended petulance, annoyance at breaking records, impatience, etc., don't get the upperhand. No amount of falls will really undo us if we keep on picking ourselves up each time. We shall be very muddy and tattered children by the time we reach home. But the bathrooms are all ready, the towels put out, and the clean clothes in the airing cupboard. The only fatal thing is to lose one's temper and give it up. It is when we notice that God is most present in us: It is the very sign of his presence.[5]

Self-control is built with a pattern of successive experiences. Self-control can be neither quickly developed nor quickly destroyed. It deserves to be carefully guarded because it will make the difference between success or failure as we face temptation.

Self-control, like the other fruit of the Spirit, doesn't develop by chance. It must be nurtured and developed day by day.

> Being confident of this, that he who began a good work in you will carry it on to completion until the day of Christ Jesus (Philippians 1:6).

Self-mastery begins when we yield ourselves to the Master, Jesus Christ. God has given each of us a life, but God will not live it for us. God has given us the power and will to enable us to live it.

Gratitude is a fruit of great cultivation; you do not find it among gross people.

—*Boswell's Tour to the Hebrides*

Somehow you and I have got to stay in touch with simplicity.

—*Thomas Howard*

10.

Building a Fortress Against Temptation

When I was living in California, I had an acquaintance who was nearly deaf. She had a habit of turning off her hearing aid when she disagreed or was bored. I do not know whether or not she realized what she was doing. However, when others saw her reach up to turn off her hearing aid, they would quickly change the subject. In a few moments she would turn the hearing aid back on.

How often we do the same thing in life—turn off the hearing aid of our minds to block out information from those we regard as insignificant. Many people in our day have deafened their ears to the wisdom of the very young or the very old, robbing themselves of significant relationships and insights from these two neglected segments of society.

When I began to discipline myself to listen to others rather than being so interested in telling them what I had to say, I found a unique world of information and inspiration, like a hidden treasure waiting for discovery. Among my first discoveries was Trudi Propach. She radiated hope. She knew exactly what to say at just the right time. Whenever I was depressed, discouraged, or perhaps burnt out, I would telephone Trudi. Something in her life encouraged me to probe for the source of her hope.

Trudi spent several trying years under the Nazi regime. Being Jewish, she faced persecution and rejection. She lost one child, victim to a brain tumor, during the war and was only rarely able to see her husband while the war raged. There were subsequent losses: home, place in society, friends, husband. Trudi was tempted to be bitter. She was tempted to gain revenge. Yet her attitudes were positive and her perspective hopeful for the future.

I found myself looking for excuses to stop by Trudi's home. I desired to know what key unlocked the door to her character, what unique virtue enabled her to see broken dreams mended. Visits to rest homes and conversations with the elderly had taught me that character, tenderness, and selflessness are not virtues that come automatically with age, but are by-products of decisions made earlier in life.

Trudi Propach had the ability to read emotions hidden from others. During one of our many conversations she said, "Harold, if you will open your eyes, you will see God-given opportunities—every day—to choose life or death. You can choose, each day and many times during each day, to live with a sense of gratitude, or give in to the temptation to be bitter. Choosing a life of gratitude is foundational to overcoming the Tempter's tactics. No one else in life can ever make that choice for you."

I felt I had heard the words of Christ, Paul the apostle, or one of the other great saints of history—Francis, Augustine, or Calvin. I added Trudi's name to the hagiography.

Trudi's life had been marked by many temptations to bitterness, hate, resentment, and self-pity. How could she say that we must choose to live with a sense of gratitude? From one perspective, she had every right to be bitter; even on that day, her aged body was steadily deteriorating. Walking away from her home, I kept reflecting on Paul's words to the church in Rome: Since "they neither glorified . . . God nor gave thanks to him, . . . their thinking became futile . . ." (Romans 1:21). Paul says that bitterness and rebellion begin, not with clenched fists, but with the refusal to have an open arm of acceptance and appreciation. Could it be that many of our battles are the result of the temptation to be ungrateful?

When Is the Proper Time to Be Grateful?

When is the right time to be grateful? Life is filled with problems, stress, anxieties, and hurts: a job loss, a divorce, terminal illness, past failures, unfair deals at work, inflation eating up savings, rebellious children, harsh and hurtful words, homes torn apart by conflict. All these are among the pressures of living in a broken world. All result from circumstances we didn't choose—the attacks of the Evil One. It is easy to wait, and wait, until we feel like giving genuine thanks. But procrastination is a choice.

There was something profound in what Trudi Propach said about choice. To choose life and express gratitude is central to overcoming temptations and building a fortress against Satan. Few people—including me—like to be reminded that choices made today determine our character tomorrow or thirty years from now.

Faced with the excruciating tension between gratitude and ingratitude, I visited the Plymouth Plantation with my children. The guides related the circumstances of the first Thanksgiving. In October 1621 the colonists decided to have a feast celebrating blessings of the year. What blessings? Hadn't they lost many members of their colony the previous year? I remembered the Thanksgiving service I attended at the Congregational Church in our village. There I was handed five grains of corn to remind me that the colonists survived on five grains of corn for days. Gratitude? They had almost starved, many in their community had died, every family had broken dreams. But the Pilgrims gave thanks.

Were the Pilgrims foolish? As I stood there at Plymouth Plantation I thought, if I had been living in 1621 I would have protested the celebration as both inappropriate and foolish. How irresponsible to share food in celebration after facing a catastrophic year of suffering. Perhaps they might have waited for a more appropriate time. Spring? No, there wouldn't be sufficient food left over from the winter. Summer? Drought might come, or perhaps unseasonably heavy rains and mildew. And of course, winter would not be the time to celebrate, because they needed what food they had to carry them through the bitter cold.

When is the appropriate time in life to be thankful? Satan will tempt us to wait. I continually meet people who say they will share gratitude with others later in life. "I will give to charities just as soon as I make more money." Paul wrote to some believers who were tempted to procrastinate about gratitude,

> There is no need for me to write to you about this service to the saints. For I know your eagerness to help, and I have been boasting about it to the Macedonians, telling them that since last year you in Achaia were ready to give; and your enthusiasm has stirred most of them to action. . . . This service that you perform is not only supplying the needs of God's people but is also overflowing in many expressions of thanks to God (2 Corinthians 9:1–2, 12).

Generosity and gratitude are inseparable; neither is complete without the other.

Every year our nation celebrates a national day of gratitude in November that we call Thanksgiving Day. Few people realize, however, that President Lincoln proclaimed a national Day of Thanksgiving just a few months after the tragic battle of Gettysburg. What an inappropriate time! The nation was in the midst of war, divided and confused. Thousands of lives had been lost. Yet the president proclaimed a national holiday of gratitude. From the viewpoint of the circumstances, as with the Pilgrims and Trudi Propach, the timing just wasn't right.

Satan will tempt us to find sufficient reasons to wait. Why? Because the appropriate time never comes.

A Unique Virtue

Gratitude is a unique virtue, standing apart from all other virtues. Truth, love, and wisdom are appropriate to desire as well as to offer to others. While wonderful in the giving, however, gratitude is poisonous when craved. Occasionally we all say, "All I want is just a little appreciation." I am not saying that we shouldn't receive appreciation. We all need expressions of it. It is one of the most powerful motivating forces known to us. Scripture calls us to build up and encourage each other. That is just another way of saying that we must demonstrate appreciation and gratitude.

But Satan tempts us to become victims of our own desires, by ingratitude. When we give in to the temptation to receive gratitude, we become victims of destructive emotional, spiritual, and psychological forces. Satan will then tempt us to calculate everything we do for others in terms of the appreciation potential. We will be in the vise of "playing to the grandstands."

How often do we "play to the grandstand"? How much kindliness can we show with no expectations of thanks? How long can we sustain thoughtfulness in the face of a thoughtless response?

What Inhibits Gratitude?

What hinders us from expressing gratitude? When I express thankfulness, I acknowledge my need for others' expressions of love and care. I become vulnerable. In showing gratitude I admit my need for you to help me solve the various crises in my life. When I say "Thank you" I show that I need what you have given to me, and I subtly admit my dependence on you for helping me to be more fully myself. This is the exact opposite of Satan's temptations to serve and worship self.

Examine the Implications

Examine the implications of saying "Thank you." "Thank you, Pastor, for the excellent sermon." Implied or assumed is an acknowledgment that someone else has insights which are helpful to you, insights which you are unable to discover on your own. When spouses say "Thank you" for a thoughtful word or gift, they are also saying, "You have something to give me, or express for me, which I need." An expression of gratitude is an expression of dependence.

Perhaps that is why the rejection of a gift is often devastating to one who has just offered it. The recipient may be saying, "I don't need you," "I am angry with you," or "Get out of my life." A rejected gift often reveals self-hate in the receiver.

A lifestyle of gratitude lowers defenses toward others, deepens relationships, and raises our defenses against Satan. That may be why people who have developed a lifestyle of gratitude are enjoyable to be around.

Myrtle Cox had been a member of our congregation for many years. Her life had been marked by many difficulties. Yet, in her presence one experienced the presence of life. I can still remember when she turned seventy. "Life is so exciting!" she exclaimed. "Just wait until you are in your seventies. You will have so many things to be thankful for, to remember, to enjoy—so many memories to recall and enjoy. It is wonderful to be alive!" Myrtle had been making choices for life for years and took a positive stance toward the future. The choice for life made her enjoyable to be with.

In expressing gratitude to God and others, I take an affirmative stance toward the future. Gratitude is a present disposition that looks back and presses forward simultaneously.

While looking out on Plymouth Bay, I began to understand the meaning of gratitude and the power it releases for overcoming temptation. In their act of thanksgiving, the Pilgrims affirmed their faith in a sovereign God. They had been sufficiently cared for in the past so as to be still alive, and they trusted that God would carry them through the next winter. Life is a bumpy road. There are potholes that jar us loose from the frameworks of our lives, potholes that Satan uses to tempt us to take protective stances toward the future: "Hold onto what you have. It is only natural," or "If you never take a risk, you'll never get hurt."

Consider the Risks

The apostle Paul took risks when he expressed gratitude to the Corinthians. They were a melting pot of problems: racial hostility, alcohol abuse, sexual immorality, false teachings, and spiritual pride. Boasting of great spirituality, they failed miserably when it came to action. They must have been an embarrassment to Paul. Yet the apostle says, "I thank my God for you. . . . God has been faithful to you." Paul's sense of gratitude opened the door to help the Corinthians resolve their serious problems. At the same time, compounding risk, he implied his need for their meager gifts.

While working toward a masters degree in psychology I was assigned to work in a halfway house. This house comprised two directors, twelve girls, and a cook. Each girl either had been arrested or was a runaway. All the girls came from upper-class, professional families. They were the most hostile group of people I have ever encountered.

My assignment was to lead group discussions weekly

for six months. Each Tuesday before I faced the Wednesday meeting, I became tense, irritable, and harsh with others. I was unpleasant to be around. After two months I was becoming ill just before the sessions. Only as I began to see within each girl the image of God, however tarnished, was I able to listen and hear, talk and be heard. When I could express appreciation for their insights, ideas, and perspectives, they in turn began to listen to what I had to offer. Gratitude enabled us to relate, and it caused the relationship to grow.

Doors to Reconciliation

Gratitude opens doors to reconciliation. The expression of gratitude invites honesty and forgiveness. Genuine appreciation creates an environment for resisting temptation, resolving conflicts, and soothing hurts. Gratitude doesn't overlook—it undergirds. Satan tempts us to overlook. Paul's gratitude, expressed to the Corinthians, was part of the foundation on which a love both tender and tough was built.

When we begin a day, a week, a new year with a deep sense of gratitude for our lives, jobs, families, and other relationships, we build fortresses against Satan. Our prayers that "God's kingdom come" should be the focus of all our praying—done with thanksgiving, as Paul reminds us. Christ's kingdom comes among us in all our everyday situations and relationships as we pray in a spirit of gratitude.

In my own family, we have tried to include in our worship a time of appreciation and gratitude, to God and to each other. It is a strong fortress against the various temptations to be bitter, resentful, and selfish. At first it was very hard for me to express appreciation to my wife, Carol, and to our children. In time I came to discover new dimensions of interest in each member of the family.

Whenever our family observes a birthday or a holiday,

or when one of us leaves for an extended period of time, we have a special little celebration of dessert and appreciation. On a birthday, everyone tells the birthday person words of appreciation. At Christmas and Thanksgiving each person takes turns listening to what the others say they like about each other: "I appreciate the fact that you love me enough to correct me." And, "Dad, I appreciate that you are not as angry as you used to be." And, "Mommy, I love you from my bottom to my heart." We have learned, incidentally, that these times need to be structured into our schedules, or we just let them pass by. Even birthday parties need planning.

Gratitude can be structured into our lives and daily routines in various ways. Buy extra thank-you notes to have on hand. Write one of those unexpected notes to a child who helped you clean up after a Sunday school class. Write notes to people who have had an impact on your life. It's a way of getting the focus off our own battles with Satan.

I have disciplined myself to write two thank-you letters for each Thanksgiving. I write them to people who made an impact on my life during my teen and college years. In one recent year I called a high-school teacher who spent many hours teaching me and five other students how to think and how to read; he also coaxed us toward appreciating good music and enjoying art. He laid the foundation for all my future education, giving me a desire to think, write, listen, and look. Now an elderly man, residing in a rest home near San Francisco, he broke into tears during my unexpected phone call. I wept too—very joyous tears. One gives, and one gets. His comment: "I thought nobody cared for me anymore. Thanks for giving me new hope." His thankful life had opened my own; my expressed gratitude so many years later opened his life to new hope.

Gratitude will begin only when we take the blinders from our eyes and express gratitude for the simple things in life given by God. This is not easy to do. Author and teacher Thomas Howard put it this way in a lecture at Gordon College:

> . . . It's difficult because we are told in a thousand talk shows and a thousand books and in every journal and seminar and in every magazine and TV ad that what we want is something else. If you drive a Pinto, what you want is a BMW. If you drive a Peugeot, you need a Mercedes. If you shop at Lechmere, you need to move up to Bergdorf and Hammacher-Schlemmer. If you go to the Cape for your holiday, you ought to try the Caribbean. If you're a mother, you ought to be an investment banker. If you work 9–5, it's a drag, and only dull people do that. If you're middle class, you need to get emancipated. Upward mobility, self-actualization, self-assertion, self-discovery, self-realization, aggression, kicks, travel, diversion, the beautiful people, radical chic—anything but where we are. Nothing could be as dull as this. But how in the world are you and I, much less the people we're going to be responsible for, going to preserve the capacity for contentment and delight in sheer unvarnished ordinariness and routine, when this is the mythology coming at us so dazzlingly?
>
> . . . The Caribbean is there, heaven knows, and it's beautiful. But have the ads for the Caribbean, with willowy women and lithe men draped languidly on the deck of somebody's 90-foot ketch with tall glasses of rum and tonic, and everyone tricked out in Nieman Marcus and Lilly Pulitzer—has that, or something like that, blunted my taste for walking through the woods? . . . Madison Avenue's doing what it can to bring this off, and they know how to administer very effective doses of their magic. Somehow you and I have got to stay in touch with simplicity.[1]

We keep busy even while we are resting. Often the television set is on, but only as background assurance that things are still happening. We avoid facing the vacuum in our lives plagued with consumeritis. Madison Avenue is bent on persuading us that the luxuries we desire are necessities. Often our cries for social equality are themselves rooted in upward mobility: equal rights with those above me. For Jesus Christ and his followers, the call to fulfillment has a totally different perspective.

> Your attitude should be the same as that of Christ Jesus:
>
> Who, being in very nature God, did not consider equality with God something to be grasped, but made himself nothing, taking the very nature of a servant, being made in human likeness (Philippians 2:5–7).

Jesus Christ did not see joy as whining equality but as intelligent sympathy, not as upward mobility but as deepened participation. His joy was true enthusiasm in the simple but profound giving of ordinary life. His was a life of gratitude.

God has created the world for our enjoyment. The Old Testament writers were filled with appreciation for God's creation. God could have made us blind to color and deaf to tones. Children, husbands, wives, parents—all have value merely because they were created by God. They are gifts. Gifts refused or distorted can be destructive. Remember the words of Paul, writing to believers:

> For although they knew God, they neither glorified him as God nor gave thanks to him. . . . Therefore God gave them over in the sinful desires of their hearts (Romans 1:21, 24).

When we fail to say "Thank you" to God, our ingratitude can be come an unverbalized form of blasphemy. Satan tempts us to bear in our personalities the marks of such blasphemy.

All the gifts we have in life are gifts on loan. In time they will all be taken away. Health can deteriorate without our choice. Family members will one by one be taken away through ill health and finally death. When I conduct the funeral of a parent, child, or grandparent, I am always struck by a recurring comment: "Oh, I wish I had told him how much I appreciated him." Isn't much of the great stress in the American family rooted in

Satan's temptation to be ungrateful to God and to each other?

Dependence and Independence

Americans pride themselves in being independent, but so does Satan. On one Fourth of July I was able to enjoy a Bostonian celebration of our nation's Declaration of Independence. Amid all the fireworks, music of the Boston Pops Orchestra, balloons, and church bells ringing, that scene of the Pilgrim Plantation came back to me. What a short memory we have! One hundred and fifty years before the signing of the Declaration of Independence, that group of settlers, coming out of tragedy and suffering, with broken dreams, did not make a declaration of independence. Instead they knelt in gratitude to declare their *dependence* on almighty God to carry them through another year. A declaration of *dependence* is where our nation began.

In New England, signs of the great culture the Pilgrims attempted to build remain. White churches dot the countryside with large, clear windows. These windows reminded the Pilgrims during worship that their whole lives were to be lived before God in gratitude. Their homes were not ticky-tacky tract homes, but durable homes expressing character and personal creativity. Town halls, commons, maple-lined streets, and quaint buildings were all built to glorify God and reflect the dignity of persons.

Monty and Betsy Burnham moved from California to pastor a church in Massachusetts. They had moved to New England six months after our move, and we became very close friends. Together we went through adjustments to long winters, cultural differences, and new avenues of ministry. Six months after their arrival, the Burnhams faced the shocking news of Betsy's terminal cancer. What happened to Monty, the two children—and to us and other friends?

During the years that followed, we all experienced the painful process of seeing Betsy deteriorate and then die in January 1982. Our two families had planned to celebrate New Year's Day together, but Betsy was taken to the hospital in December to face the final days of her life. We decided to celebrate New Year's Day together in the hospital. Celebrate? We spent time together talking about friends she wanted to see when she went to be with Christ. I was scheduled to leave for Europe in a few days, and we knew this would be our last time together as couples.

My wife, Carol, said, "Betsy, I want to tell you how much I have appreciated your friendship." That statement opened a door of love. We spent the next hour thanking each other, laughing together, reflecting on the adjustments we had all made in moving to New England. We closed by relating what we appreciated in each other. Then we held hands, told each other good-by, wept, and prayed. I can still remember the closing words of Betsy's prayer: "Thank you, Jesus, for another day to live. Thank you for my friends, my husband, my family, and my life. Amen."

Wasn't that an inappropriate time to pray such a prayer? She was leaving her husband, a successful marriage, a rewarding ministry in Newton, and two teenage daughters. Yes, she had been tempted to be bitter. But instead she was grateful: "Thank you for another day of life. . . ."

As we drove toward our home, Carol and I talked about our weak understanding as Protestants of the communion of saints. During our conversation I remembered the words of Jesus Christ on the evening of his arrest and deep distress—words of thankfulness and communion: "And when he had given thanks, he broke it and said, 'This is my body, which is for you . . .'" (1 Corinthians 11:24).

Jesus Christ chose to express gratitude at the most inappropriate time. This was the night in which he was betrayed! With the ultimate sacrifice in full view, Christ reversed Adam's choice. Adam ate food in rebellion and was expelled from the garden. Christ offered food as an act of reconciliation and entered a garden of anguish and rejection. In the face of all that coming pain, Christ took the bread, and when he broke it, he gave thanks! From a human perspective, the timing was off. Shouldn't he have waited until the Resurrection?

The Greek word *eucharist,* which the church has called Communion throughout its history, means the Great Thanksgiving. This is what lies behind our coming to the table of our Lord. We proclaim a great thanksgiving, remembering the suffering of Christ, and we keep on proclaiming it until he comes again. This is where we find the foundation for building a fortress to withstand temptation, in all its forms—in the expression of gratitude.

And surely I am with you always, to the very end of the age.

—Jesus Christ of Nazareth

He said to me, "My grace is sufficient for you, for my power is made perfect in weakness."

—Paul of Tarsus

11.

Living in the World —But Not of It

Popular concepts of ungodliness limit it to whatever is immoral, depraved, debased, dishonest, or the like. To the person facing a war with temptation, there is a tendency to conclude that he or she is ungodly. This attitude intensifies the struggles within. It is important to note that much that is highly moral, cultured, and refined is as ungodly as murder, hate, or any other immoral act.

The word *ungodly* simply means "not having regard for God." It is the breaking of the first commandment. Ungodliness includes all that is done without taking God into account. A person fighting spiritual battles with temptation may be the most godly person in the world. The issue is, are you placing God at the center of the struggle? If you are, *you are godly* and have kept the first commandment: "You shall have no other gods before me" (Exodus 20:3). Every act in our lives that does not take God into account is an act of ungodliness. The power to overcome the forces of evil are found in the act of placing God at the center of our lives, including our struggles.

History records many great accomplishments by the human family made possible only because of God's "common grace." However, these deeds in themselves may be beneficial for the race; but because God has been left out of these accomplishments, the works are made ungodly. What measures up to high moral standards is not always godly, although godliness will express itself in moral behavior. The world's religions, cults, and political ideologies all have moral codes, but conformity to them can be worldliness.

> . . . since what may be known about God is plain to them, because God has made it plain to them. For since the creation of the world God's invisible qualities—his eternal power and divine nature—have been clearly seen, being understood from what has been made, so that men are without excuse.
>
> For although they knew God, they neither glorified him as God nor gave thanks to him, but their thinking became futile and their foolish hearts were darkened. Although they claimed to be wise, they became fools and exchanged the glory of the immortal God for images made to look like mortal man and birds and animals and reptiles (Romans 1:19–23).

As morality in itself is not a guarantee of godliness, neither is love.

> If you love those who love you, what credit is that to you? Even "sinners" love those who love them. And if you do good to those who are good to you, what credit is that to you? Even "sinners" do that (Luke 6:32–33).

The heathen have a knowledge of God and unbelievers can love, but neither is godliness. Godliness is placing God at the center of our lives. Paul stated it succinctly when he said, "Whatever you do, do it *all* for the glory of God" (1 Corinthians 10:31, italics mine). That little word "all" includes our battles with temptation.

Faith is not simply trusting God to do things we ask of him; it is trusting God with each aspect of our lives.

Can Christians be ungodly? Of course! Paul encouraged the Christians at Rome to "offer yourselves to God, as those who have been brought from death to life; and offer the parts of your body to him as instruments of righteousness" (Romans 6:13). "Offer" is the key word to godliness and overcoming the world. The work of the Holy Spirit in our hearts is not an unconscious or automatic thing. Our wills and intelligence must yield to and cooperate with the benign intentions of God. The New Testament records workings of the Spirit through people's choices and responses. Watchfulness, prayer, self-discipline, and study are indispensable to any real progress of overcoming.

To Flee or to Be Separate?

Those who seek solutions to the problem of temptation have often coupled, for better and for worse, two biblical ideas: to *flee* temptation, and to *be separate* from the world. But how are they different, and which is better or worse?

Since the time of Christ, sincere Christians have constructed walls to protect themselves from the intrusions of the world outside. The attempts have varied in method, depending on the definition of "worldliness." Cloister walls have been used like fortresses to separate one from family and friends. Vows of silence have been taken to bridle gossip and lying tongues. Abstinence from certain foods and beverages has been the cry of some. Celibacy has been widespread, sometimes carried to the extreme of self-castration. In our own generation, however, most choose less severe and painful paths: we have devised lists of forbidden pleasures as measures of safety and standards of orthodoxy.

Many of these attempts to flee temptation through separation from the "world" are not intrinsically misguided. But however much distance we put between ourselves and the "world," the self cannot be escaped. Cloister walls will not shut out the imagination. Pledges against certain beverages and entertainments cannot ward off the intrusion of lust, greed, envy, and hate. However far we flee, or however completely we separate, the self is there. If we understand and accept this truth, it can help to set us free from unbiblical and always disappointing attempts to *merely* flee "the whole mess," or to *simply* separate ourselves from a world "going to hell."

The separation solution is too simplistic. It tries to remove all tensions and battles from a Christian's life. It denies reality and neglects the fundamental issue of ungodliness.

But how do we live *in* the world while not being *of* the world? To flee temptation by withdrawing from the world all too often leads to a neglect of the very world—including ourselves—that needs Christ's redemption. Jesus calls us to live and follow him—in a world dominated by ungodliness. Physical removal from the world is therefore delusive and destructive, since our battles with temptation, ungodliness, and worldliness are within. The apostle Paul writes,

> For our struggle is not against flesh and blood, but against the rulers, against the authorities, against the powers of this dark world and against the spiritual forces of evil in the heavenly realms (Ephesians 6:12).

Neither "withdrawal nor the fear of punishment will restrain one from sin," warns John Calvin.[1]

"The world according to Garp," in John Irving's best-selling novel of that title, is a world where tomfoolery and chaos can be observed only by apparently foolish seers like Garp who attempt, in a rough-hewn way, to overcome the world's disorder with some kind of moral order. The apostles John and Paul provide a similar though profoundly richer and truer view of the world.

For John, the "normal" world of moral chaos is not to be ignored, but rather overcome. Anyone remade in God's image, says John, has overcome the world. "This is the victory that has overcome the world, even our faith" (1 John 5:4).

Sin and holiness are related to the object of our faith, that which we live for and worship. "Who is it that overcomes the world?" asks John. "Only he who believes that Jesus is the Son of God" (1 John 5:5). How so? Our belief "in" (not "about") Jesus reorients us and gives us a redemptive perspective as a leverage against this world.

Throughout history, believers have built places of worship where the faithful could gather to worship and celebrate the victory of Christ over all idols and forces of evil. The weekly gatherings reminded them of Christ's victory and nourished them.

When societies forsake this act of worship, they always create substitutes. Think of Sunday football, for an obvious example. I am not against football, but I wonder if in some sense the Astrodome isn't our Notre Dame, or the Orange Bowl our Westminster. Are the Dallas Cowboys cheerleaders becoming substitute saints for our children, cheering them toward gods of fame, money, and sensuality? Do advertisements offer immediate gains in place of the groans and fruits of the one Spirit who is holy? Tertullian, an early church father, assailed the early Christians for attending gladiatorial meets. Because he was against sports? No. He was concerned that Christians were subtly lured into a form of idolatry.

Idolatry is subtle and at the core of all worldliness and ungodliness. When do football, TV, music, money, or simply "more" of anything become part of what John calls "the passing world"? Listen to what distinguishes the *passing* world:

> You must not love this passing world or anything that is in this world . . . because nothing the world has to offer—
> the *sensual* body,
> the *lustful* eye,

pride in possessions—
could ever come from the Father.
(1 John 2:15–16 JERUSALEM BIBLE)

The body, the eye, and possessions are not "the *passing* world." The world that most needs to be overcome is the world of self-made gods. The passing world worships the body as merely sensual; its eye has become lustful. The passing world worships the self by adoring self's acquisitions. This world of sensuality, envy, and pride starts within us.

Idolatry is a natural phenomenon. It lies at the core of our struggles. The world that passes is "normal." We grow up with this frame of mind. "In the early years of childhood," Earl Jabay writes, "we form our idols without much awareness. But when we come to adulthood, it is time to put away the fantasies we have about ourselves and live in the real world which God has created."[2]

Paul said, "When I became a man, I put childish ways behind me" (1 Corinthians 13:11). This is where true separation begins. Jabay uses Paul as an example:

> Paul is perhaps the prime example of a person who could not rid himself of overwhelming guilt feelings until he gave up the idol of himself as one righteous through the Pharisaic law of men and substituted the image and likeness of Christ in its place. This is what Paul meant when he said, "I through the law died to the law, that I might live to God. I have been crucified with Christ; I no longer live, but Christ lives in me" [Galatians 2:19–20].[3]

Every person grows up clinging to the self, insisting that *this* self is the world's center.

The ultimate pull of the passing world is not primarily in the momentary lure of pleasures and power. Rather, the problem is its creation of gods in one's own image: the world according to me.

Serving self through its own idols yields a domain of darkness. Yielding to Christ brings the harmony of a new world, a kingdom of light. Yielding to the true God is to say *yes* to the intended goal for myself.

At the moment we decide to follow Christ in faith as Savior and Lord, the real call begins. Our personal lives become battlefields of belief, values, and purpose. The lines of battle are revealed in Christ's last prayer for the churches recorded by John.

> My prayer is not that you take them out of the world but that you protect them from the evil one. They are not of the world, even as I am not of it. Sanctify them by the truth; your word is truth. As you sent me into the world, I have sent them into the world. For them I sanctify myself, that they too may be truly sanctified (John 17:15–19).

Becoming sanctified is becoming set apart—in relationship to God and to our god-intended selves.

We need God's protection because He does not call us out of the world. In fact, God puts us into the world, just as Christ was placed in the world. And that's how Jesus prayed—and lived.

Life Is Relationships

Did Jesus withdraw? Absolutely not! He entered more fully into the joy and sorrow of human existence than anyone else. Jesus came to bring redemption. What did He come to redeem us to and from?

You might answer, "Christ came to redeem us from sin." But what is sin? What do you think of when you hear the word sin: drugs? murder? lying? lust? greed? No. Sin goes much deeper than these things.

One day while trying to describe sin to my children, it suddenly dawned on me that it can be defined primarily as an attitude of rebellion against relationships—our relationships with God, ourselves, and others. Since the fall of Adam, human beings have found it difficult to have relationships that satisfy. The courts of the nation bear witness to our inability to get along with one another.

Life is relationships. As human beings, we cannot live without being involved with others. All people are engaged in a network of relatedness. Relationships profoundly affect the quality of life. If our relationships are good, our lives tend to be filled with joy and satisfaction. If they are bad, our inner sense of satisfaction leaves. God created us to have relationships that enrich our lives. He hates whatever undermines and destroys human relationships.

All of us can testify to times when we have experienced misunderstandings in relationships. It is hard to say "I am sorry" or "It was my fault." It is so much easier to turn out the lights, to pretend nothing has happened, and so avoid the issue. Why? Because our sinful nature rebels against the give-and-take of true relationships.

The Urge to Rebel

In a marriage we may be tempted to blame, accuse, and walk away from the pressure. To own up to our part in a problem is sometimes harder than any physical challenge. Why is it so hard to say, "Let's forgive each other and work this out"? To forgive and to offer forgiveness is to check that rebellious urge to rule over the other—to control and so to destroy the relationship.

On occasion, I sense a special need to spend time with my children, yet I suddenly find myself tired and disinterested in their problems. I avoid them. If a friend stops by unexpectedly, however, the tiredness leaves and my God-given responsibility of parenting is quickly forgotten. Why? Because in my sinful nature I am at that moment rebelling against serving my children. Rather than offering them the seeds of character and self-esteem through my interested attention, I am tempted to ignore them because of my self-centeredness. What, after all, can they do for *me* right now, for my need to be a lord? My friend can feed my ego at the moment in a way the children cannot.

Children require time—great quantities of time. There can be no quality time without the sacrifice of time itself. In the kind of situation I have described, my temptation is to take a shortcut to personal gratification at the expense of a relationship in which I may receive no immediate thanks, let alone praise. "Praise *me* . . ." goes the dusty tune of our hearts.

The Ten Commandments Are Relational

In the past I thought of the Ten Commandments as ten *don'ts* designed to keep me from being free. They are not. They are affirmations of value and dignity. They spell out how we can best be fulfilled as persons. They affirm relationships.

The three relational dimensions central to these commandments are our relationships to God, to our neighbors, and to ourselves. They are expressed very directly. God says not *my people* shall, but *you* shall.

> I am the LORD your God, who brought you out of Egypt, out of the land of slavery.
> You shall have no other gods before me.
> You shall not make for yourself an idol in the form of anything in heaven above or on the earth beneath or in the waters below. You shall not bow down to them or worship them; for I, the LORD your God, am a jealous God, punishing the children for the sin of the fathers to the third and fourth generation of those who hate me, but showing love to a thousand generations of those who love me and keep my commandments.
> You shall not misuse the name of the LORD your God, for the LORD will not hold anyone guiltless who misuses his name (Exodus 20:2–7).

These commandments are set within the framework of God's sovereign grace. God desires to bring us out of our slavery and bondage. The commandments begin with God's self-revelation. The revelation of God's sovereign grace gives us foundation for self-discovery. Self-knowledge is found in the discovery of who God is. God's definition of reality and sovereign grace free us to be truly human and relational. It is God's grace that enables us to face his guidelines and absolutes for relationships. These commandments affirm relationships and negate sin. Sin can be defined in this context as a rebellion against relationships. The other major outworking of sin is the desire to have power over others and control others in nonrelational, manipulative, and exploitive ways.

A major factor in our struggles with temptation is the urge to exploit relationships. All temptations are variations on the Evil One's basic ploy. From idolatry springs all manner of broken relationships.

Many sermons on temptation are "how-to-do-it": "Six Easy Steps to Resisting Temptation," or—and this title is a classic—"Nuclear Power Over Temptation Through Fasting." All overlook the central issue: temptation is not just the lure of coins jingling in our pockets, the opposite sex flocking at our heels, or someone applauding us in public. When we live with our own gods we live in fear. We need the jingles, the interested looks, and the applause. Only a relationship with God will challenge these fears that lead to death.

Notice the rich development and the dignity of relationships expressed in the following commandments:

> Remember the Sabbath day by keeping it holy. Six days you shall labor and do all your work, but the seventh day is a Sabbath to the LORD your God. On it you shall not do any work, neither you, nor your son or daughter, nor your manservant or maidservant, nor your animals, nor the alien within your gates. For in six days the LORD made the heavens and the earth, the sea, and all that is in them, but

he rested on the seventh day. Therefore the LORD blessed the Sabbath day and made it holy (Exodus 20:8–11).

The Sabbath was given to protect the human community from exhaustion and exploitation. In God's eyes, our worth comes above the state and all systems that seek to diminish our dignity. People are not machines to be "worked" for the sake of productivity. The echo rings back from the mountains of creation: All have worth. Even nature and animals are not to be exploited.

Humanity's dignity is that of our God. The opposite of the temptation that gives way to sin and death is an adventure that brings life. Sin reduces us to a mere shell of self. God's life expands us to a point of abundance that overflows with life for others.

Who is my neighbor, and where is my neighborhood?

> Hearing that Jesus had silenced the Sadducees, the Pharisees got together. One of them, an expert in the law, tested him with this question: "Teacher, which is the greatest commandment in the Law?"
>
> Jesus replied: " 'Love the Lord your God with all your heart and with all your soul and with all your mind.' This is the first and greatest commandment. And the second is like it: 'Love your neighbor as yourself.' All the Law and the Prophets hang on these two commandments" (Matthew 22:34–40).
>
> Honor your father and your mother, so that you may live long in the land the LORD your God is giving you" (Exodus 20:12).

Where does our neighborhood begin? Who are my neighbors that I am called to love? My parents? True neighborliness begins with those who know me for who I really am.

Why the home first? Our relationships with our families reveal our true selves. In our weaknesses and our strengths we are called to honor, first of all, those closest to us. To honor is to submit, in service:

> Be very careful, then, how you live—not as unwise, but as wise, making the most of every opportunity, because the days are evil. Therefore do not be foolish, but understand what the Lord's will is. Do not get drunk on wine, which leads to debauchery. Instead, be filled with the Spirit. Speak to one another with psalms, hymns and spiritual songs. Sing and make music in your heart to the Lord, always giving thanks to God the Father for everything, in the name of our Lord Jesus Christ.
>
> Submit to one another out of reverence for Christ (Ephesians 5:15–21).

The apostle Paul speaks of the infilling of the Holy Spirit. What is the first thing the Holy Spirit inspires—evangelism? emotional highs? meditation? devotional life? No. The Holy Spirit first of all brings restoration to those estranged from God, from neighbor, and from themselves. These are the relationships designed in creation, affirmed in the Ten Commandments, and restored through God's grace.

Love of God is godliness. Love of neighbor is neighborliness. This theme continues to expand like a Bach fugue, touching every aspect of proper neighborliness.

> You shall not murder.
>
> You shall not commit adultery.
>
> You shall not steal.
>
> You shall not give false testimony against your neighbor (Exodus 20:13–16).

Here we discover a rich concert of fulfilled relationships. The protection of fragile relationships is central to each of these commandments. People are not to be used; godliness and neighborliness mean to honor, not to use. How easily—how naturally—husbands and wives can refuse to communicate, children sass, believers gossip, and employers exploit.

Using others is the natural warding off of fear and insecurity. We use others to make ourselves lords. We *use*—or, if that isn't immediately possible—we *covet*—such use:

> You shall not covet your neighbor's house. You shall not covet your neighbor's wife, or his manservant or maidservant, his ox or donkey, or anything that belongs to your neighbor (Exodus 20:17).

Glossy magazine ads and television commercials often encourage unhealthful competition, ingratitude, and exploitation. They frequently tempt us to covet. To covet is to diminish our God-given dignity.

We do not trust God, so we fear; we fear, so we use or covet others and others' possessions. This dark spiral removes us from the personal dignity intended by God.

A Good Discovery

Discovering God's love enables us to discover our neighbors' worth. Unfortunately, sometimes a keen understanding and appreciation of the Ten Commandments can nevertheless cloud their essential point. This was the problem with the Pharisee who was testing Jesus in the story we looked at earlier. Jesus told him to "love God and love your neighbor." The integrity of relationships rests on the Creation, the Ten Commandments, and the love-word of Jesus. True dignity rests on the bedrock of a love for God and a love for neighbor mirroring a proper valuation of oneself. Each of us is called back to restoring the very likeness of God. The goal of redemption is restored relationships.

The Armor of God

To conquer temptation, we need to understand how sin operates. The battle is against forces of evil that seek to destroy all relationships. The apostle Paul warns us that we struggle because our battle is not with flesh and blood—not a contending with other people—but against the forces and ruler of darkness. These forces of evil always dehumanize, produce discouragement, cause confusion, and ignite self-centeredness.

Paul tells us, however, that there is hope. We can conquer these forces. We can overcome temptation by "putting on the whole armor of God."

> Finally, be strong in the Lord and in the strength of his might. Put on the whole armor of God, that you may be able to *stand against the wiles of the devil.* For we are not contending against flesh and blood, but against the principalities, against the powers, against the world rulers of this present darkness, against the spiritual hosts of wickedness in the heavenly places. Therefore take the whole armor of God, that you may be able to *withstand in the evil day,* and having done all, to stand. *Stand therefore,* having girded your loins with truth, and having put on the breastplate of righteousness, and having shod your feet with the equipment of the gospel of peace; above all, taking the shield of faith, with which you can quench all the flaming darts of the evil one. And take the helmet of salvation, and the sword of the Spirit, which is the word of God. Pray at all times in the Spirit, with all prayer and supplication. To that end keep alert with all perseverance, making supplication for all the saints (Ephesians 6:10–18 RSV, italics mine).

These figures of speech tell us something about our faith, our battles, and our victories. Note the expressions "having girded" our loins with truth, "having put on" the breastplate of righteousness, and "having shod" our feet with the equipment of the gospel of peace. The verbs all denote something done in the past. This happened when we made the decision to place our total lives under the lordship of Jesus Christ.

All the pieces of armor, except for the helmet, provide protection only for the front of the soldier. The implication is that soldiers were expected to face their conflicts head-on. It is when they turned their backs on conflicts that they were most vulnerable to the enemy's attacks.

Equipped and Ready

This equipment assures us of readiness. The imperative command "be strong" assumes that we are weak: you do not say "be strong" to strong people. Thus, Paul indicates, God gives us protection and preparation in our weakness. We are equipped for all the battles that will continually confront us.

The order of listing the armor is significant. First, we are to gird ourselves with the belt of truth. The belt keeps all the pieces of the armor together. The soldier hangs everything on his belt. This belt is the truth about ourselves. The biggest battle in life is to accept the truth about ourselves. It is honestly facing ourselves that enables us to accept God's sovereign grace.

Second, Christ gives us the breastplate of righteousness, which protects the heart—the place of the emotions. Living in the shadow of the Fall brings discouragements, feelings of insecurity, and self-condemnation. Emotions can manipulate and deceive us. We are guarded from being condemned by false guilt, from being controlled by our moods.

Next, our feet are to be shod with the equipment of the gospel of peace. Shoes are essential to fighting any battle. Picture the first-century soldier dressed in armor but without shoes. Soon unpaved roads, thorns, and pebbles will bruise and cut the feet. Roman soldiers had cleats attached to the bottom of their shoes to enable them to stand firmly, not losing their footing. They were able to maintain stability when attacked.

Paul next describes the shield of faith. There is no great virtue in faith, for everyone has faith in something. The relativist has faith that there are no absolutes. The atheist has faith that there is no God (even though the title is dependent on the word *theist,* implying godship). The secular humanist has faith that humankind will evolve to goodness—contrary to all the historical evidence. So for the Christian, it is the object of faith that is important.

A shield was a complementary piece of armor, adaptable and movable because it was not attached to the body. This enabled the soldier to move it for each battle condition. Roman shields ranged from two to four feet tall. A soldier would position the shield so as to reflect sunlight into the eyes of the enemy. Paul says that the shields are useful for extinguishing "flaming arrows," or in the words of the King James Version, "fiery darts." It was common in the first century to dip the tips of arrows in pitch and then set them aflame. These darts could bring panic and cause the soldiers to lose their footing.

Next Paul tells us to take the "sword of the Spirit," which he defines as the Word of God. A sword was tangible, concrete, objective, and solid. Note that the Holy Spirit and the Word are connected in this word picture. Yielding to the Spirit is yielding to Scripture. This is important because in this way we are protected from all forms of manipulation that is framed in spiritual language. Satan's first temptation on humanity was an appeal to be "spiritual": "You will be like God." Jesus, the Second Adam, was tempted by spiritual language. He was tempted to sidestep conflict and to seek miracles rather than obedience.

Last, Paul tells us to take the "helmet of salvation." The helmet was designed to protect the head—that is, the mind, the intelligence, the ability to reason and think. It is the mind that sends the messages to the body to inform the various parts how to act and respond when there is a problem. The memory of Christ's love and recalling God's Word can protect us from mental confusion and darkness. Our minds were designed to think God's thoughts after him. Jesus came to take away our sins, not our minds. He does not eradicate the mind, but regenerates and redeems it.

Paul also calls us to pray. Prayer is not a piece of armor, but it is essential to the fight. Prayer is to follow understanding. It is an action that verifies everything we believe about the universe. It is not just a psychological exercise, an act of magic, or getting in touch with "spiritual energy."

Paul says we are to pray "in the Spirit." According to the passage, in which the "sword of the Spirit" is equated with the Word of God, we are encouraged to pray within the context of God's Word. When emotions are down, we can pray and be assured that God is present, because Scripture affirms this truth.

Writing from prison, Paul does not ask for prayer that God will change his circumstances, but God will change him. Consider why he says this. It is possible to understand all the armor—that is, have correct doctrine—put on all the armor, and still succumb to sin. Why? We tend to forget that we live in a supernatural universe. God is present to help us, equip us, and encourage us in our battles against temptation. However, God does not always change our circumstances. As a child I used to have a little sign hanging over my bedroom door: "Prayer changes things." The sign was only a half-truth. The complete truth can best be stated, "Prayer changes people." God desires to change us, even when external conditions and circumstances do not change.

Putting on the armor—even the whole armor—is not sufficient without prayer. We are to commune with and relate to God, that primary relationship.

Paul instructed believers to build this defense because it does not happen by osmosis. He knew that believers could fail to stand, could fail in the face of temptation, and could often forget that the primary battle is not with flesh and blood, but is a spiritual one.

Holding Our Ground

It is noteworthy that the apostle says *stand* rather than *fight.* This word "stand" suggests the intensity of a battle with temptation. Against the forces of evil arrayed against us, "holding our ground" may be the only thing we can do.

What do we do when we are discouraged by battles with temptation? What do we do when we are drained spiritually? What do we do when we face struggles with ungodliness, worldliness, and temptations to sin? Fight? No. A fight will drain our will. To fight the temptation may intensify it. We must refuse to move and refuse to ponder the issues anymore. Stand still until the attacks diminish.

Those who learn to stand make the defeat of Satan possible. The Devil will be defeated by our standing on what God has said. One day the struggle will end. It will end for all of us either at the end of our lives or at the return of Jesus Christ. We start by remembering who we are, what we are, and who Jesus Christ is. We continue by reminding ourselves that God is not ashamed to call us children. When we put on these truths, the battle is all but over.

Become familiar with these pieces of armor. Exercise them daily. Practice thinking about them in the face of every temptation. And above all, do not give up if there is no immediate change in circumstances. Paul reminds us that the attacks may be there a long time. That's why he states, "Having done all, *stand.*" When we persevere in the face of our battles and besetting sins, we are doing the right thing—we are godly. God promised that if we "resist the devil . . . he will flee from [us]" (James 4:7).

Give gifts freely and for nothing, that others may profit by them and fare well because of you and your goodness. In this way you shall be truly good and Christian.

—*Martin Luther*

The kingdom of God is not a matter of talk, but of power.

—*Paul of Tarsus*

12.

Experience Your Future in the Present

Jerry, a man in his forties, had just overcome a serious problem that had plagued him for more than twenty years. Through the help of his pastor and a clinical psychologist he was able to defeat it. However, Jerry was in for a rude awakening. He soon discovered there were other serious temptations facing him. His life during the previous years had been consumed battling his plaguing difficulty with drugs. He began to struggle with depression and discouragement as he encountered a whole new set of temptations.

Two factors lay at the root of Jerry's disillusionment. First, over the years he had dealt with life in terms of immediate, daily struggles. Second, he had built expectations that he would achieve a level plateau of spirituality once his drug problem was conquered. He assumed that this new spirituality would free him from struggles with the world. His pastor and counselor had failed to give him a larger picture of the Christian's walk.

Caught Between Two Kingdoms

We fight the forces of evil at work in ourselves, in other people, and in society at large. Why is the Christian life such a painful struggle? Because we are caught between two kingdoms—the kingdom of this world and the kingdom of God. It is on this battlefield that we face and will continue to face temptations daily. Like Jerry, our daily battles with temptation can blind us to the larger reality of God's kingdom. When this happens, our scope can become narrow and bind us in a strait jacket of our circumstances. The Bible offers a view of reality that shows the believer facing these battles realistically and victoriously.

Paul called us to "fight the good fight." At the core of every battle with temptation lies this conflict between these two kingdoms. Jesus' teaching on the kingdom of God challenged the "gods of this world," and people understood the issues. His teaching aroused resentment, irritation, hostility, and rage in some of the hearers. His teaching compelled other, responsive listeners to focus on power beyond themselves. His kingdom is described as one that, like the mustard seed in the parable, grows slowly but surely among all the flourishing weeds of this world's kingdom.

Jesus promised that joy and peace would continue unabated through all the troubles and pitfalls that lay ahead. "In this world you will have trouble. But take heart! I have overcome the world" (John 16:33). Christ overcame the world, not by negating all conflict—his life proved quite the contrary—but by revealing its true nature. Jesus' kingdom is not a utopia. He calls us to test eternity in time, to experience new life in the midst of the kingdom of this world.

Christ's teaching about this kingdom involves both the future and the present. It is concerned with the choice to serve, to care, to overcome sin, and to resist evil in all its forms. His kingdom is the environment in which we express his authority. The word "kingdom" does not consist primarily of a geographical territory, but rather the reign and sovereignty of a ruler. George Ladd explains, "The primary meaning of both the Hebrew word *malkuth* in the Old Testament and of the Greek word *basileia* in the New Testament is the rank, authority and sovereignty exercised by a King."[1]

When we pray "thy kingdom come," we are not praying for heaven to come to earth. We are praying for Christ's will to be done on earth as faithfully as it is in heaven. That assumes there will be conflict. Ladd defines the kingdom as "the realm in which God's reign may be experienced. But again, the biblical facts are not simple. Sometimes the Bible speaks of the Kingdom as the realm into which we enter at present, sometimes as though it were future."[2]

> But if I drive out demons by the Spirit of God, then the kingdom of God has come upon you (Matthew 12:28).
>
> For if you do these things, you will never fail, and you will receive a rich welcome into the eternal kingdom of our Lord . . . (2 Peter 1:10–11).
>
> Jesus replied, "The kingdom of God does not come with your careful observation, nor will people say, 'Here it is,' or 'There it is,' because the kingdom of God is within you" (Luke 17:20–21).
>
> They will tell of the glory of your kingdom
>   and speak of your might,
> so that all men may know of your mighty acts
>   and the glorious splendor of your kingdom.
> Your kingdom is an everlasting kingdom,
>   and your dominion endures through all generations.
> (Psalm 145:11–13)

Whether present or future, God's kingdom implies the reign of God's power in our lives. Our battle with temptation is ultimately rooted in this conflict between the kingdom of this world and the kingdom of Jesus Christ. Victory is won by allowing God's sovereign control to be apparent in our lives.

When this is realized, the meaning becomes clear. The kingdom is not a realm of just people, but of God's reign in people both individually and collectively. John Bright writes, "The Kingdom of God is not only the goal of all history and the reward of all believers, not only the norm by which all human behavior is judged; it is a new order which even now bursts in upon the present one and summons us to be its people."[3]

If this, then, is the Christian's situation, we need to ask what part we play in the life of the world. Is it just to witness, to evangelize, to lead the Christian life? It is all these things, but it includes more. With every generation, the kingdom either enlarges or diminishes in proportion to the number of people who are submissive to Christ's rule in their lives. Each time we stand against temptation, fight evil, reach out to the poor, seek justice, or honor God's rule, we expand the kingdom of God.

This gives us a new perspective on temptation. The focus is off our present battles and placed within the context of a larger reality, a reality beyond this present material world. The kingdom is at work in the midst of our battles with temptation on the job, in the home, or in some church-related ministry.

When we lose a battle with temptation and give in to our sinful desires, it means that Satan has succeeded in persuading us to choose another kingdom. The goals and values we express when we lose a battle mark us as citizens of this other, earthly kingdom. But each time we stand against temptation and choose to follow Christ, we enlarge God's kingdom.

This hope of the kingdom should motivate us. We don't resist temptation for our sakes alone. We are engaged in the adventure of all things being made new. Our present lifestyles are to reflect joy, peace, love and truth—in such simple acts as expressing gratitude to the gasoline attendant, showing genuine concern for an unbelieving neighbor, standing against evil in the community, and in loving our families. When this happens, the kingdom of God expands.

Years ago, when the British colonized various parts of the world, they brought with them the values of their empire. People living in one of the colonies would understand much about London, purely from observation, even though they might never have the opportunity to go there. They would know all about having a "spot of tea." Why? Because the colonizers reflected the values and lifestyle of another kingdom.

We are to be colonizers and representatives of Christ's kingdom. As we reflect the customs and manners of his kingdom, people should know where our citizenship lies. Every time we stand against sin, take people seriously, or give a cup of cold water in the name of the King, we display the hope of that future kingdom.

To all the citizens of his kingdom Jesus entrusted the responsibility to be light in the midst of darkness, salt in the midst of decay, and lambs among wolves. The peace he promised us does not mean an absence of conflict. Our goals are not to be centered on our painful battles with temptation, but on the hope of that future kingdom and on the expansion of that kingdom in the present reality.

A friend once sent me a book about faith. The book remarked that faith in God guarantees success, health, and financial wealth. Are these the primary goals of God's kingdom? Shortly after I received the book I was listening to a Christian talk program on which the host stated, "We are citizens of that future kingdom, and since heaven's streets are paved with gold, God wants only the best for all of us. We must all 'claim by faith' Cadillacs, mink coats, diamond rings, the best homes, and expect nothing less than a top salary." Immediately I asked myself, "By what standards do we measure God's blessing and our citizenship in God's kingdom?"

With these issues in my mind, I found myself leading a group of sixty Gordon College students and leaders on a missions project to the Dominican Republic. While helping a local pastor, who lived with his family in a shack consisting of branches of tropical plants covered with banana leaves, these issues began to be resolved. I began to understand what it means to be an ambassador of this future-yet-present kingdom, to live with the tension as an alien seeking to enlarge the domain. This man of God, lacking in formal education and deceptively strong despite his malnourished body, radiated God's love.

Possessing little, this pastor was rich. Are we to believe that the pastor lacked faith because he lives in a culture where economic advancement is next to impossible? Were his simple hut, lack of transportation, and used clothing all signs that he has not been blessed by God? Should he have been praying for a Cadillac and a palatial home?

Observing this pastor and his congregation gave me a new perspective on God's domain. The pastor's life was an incarnation of the biblical vision of enlarging God's kingdom. It gave me a new power to cope with the struggles and temptations which I battle daily. My own vision concerning the kingdom of God, I realized, had been blinded by Western values and electronic "Hee Haw" Christianity. The kingdom of God, the faith, the gospel, and the Christian life cannot, and must not, be measured by distorted standards of spiritual success.

When we first arrived in the Dominican Republic, we began our mission by taking a walk through the village where we were going to build a church for this congregation. The village had no roads, only dirt paths. Earlier there had been a tremendous rainstorm, and the paths were slick with mud and clay. As the group came by a simple hut, a young girl—a member of the congregation there—took one of our team members by the hand and led her into her yard of mud. This vibrant child of Christ took this family's "gold"—their water (which her mother had walked three miles to get, since the water in the streams and wells are contaminated)—knelt in the mud, and washed the student's sneakers with her family's only drinking water supply. The mother and her children knew something about the blessings of faith that many of us fail to see. God's kingdom is enlarged through service given in love. It has little to do with material things.

I often reflect on the whole episode and wonder if there isn't another perspective on those "streets of gold." I frequently recall the scene of that eleven-year-old girl kneeling in the mud to wash a pair of sneakers.

Meanwhile, back in the Kingdom of Madison Avenue, with its slick magazine ads, billboards, and catchy jingles, I realize more clearly than ever that you and I are continually tempted in subtle ways to walk on people in order to get what we want.

Perhaps the gold in that future kingdom will be a dirt road, the thing we walk on, the lowest common denominator. Heaven, the ultimate expression of the kingdom of God, is the place of restored and reconciled relationships. Because Jesus is King, and when this King reigns, relationships and service are primary.

We pray, "Thy kingdom come, thy will be done on earth as it is in heaven." The confidence that this prayer will be answered when God brings human history to its divinely ordained consummation enables the Christian to retain balance and sanity in this mad world in which we live.

Ever since my experience in the Dominican Republic, I find myself thinking differently each Sunday when the people of God pray, "Thy kingdom come, thy will be done on earth as it is in heaven." Personal struggles with temptation, battles of the will, the allure of power all seem trivial when I realize that the King calls all of us to enlarge his kingdom through obedience and service. Sometimes I find myself speechless, unable to pray those words, because the memory of the glow on the little girl's face keeps shining, leaving me with only an unspoken "Thank you, God."

The apostle John, who described those heavenly streets of gold, addressed a group of believers who thought they had great faith. He wrote, "You say, 'I am rich; I have acquired wealth and do not need a thing.' But you do not realize that you are wretched, pitiful, poor, blind and naked. I counsel you to buy from me gold refined in the fire, so you can become rich; and white clothes to wear, so you can cover your shameful nakedness; and salve to put on your eyes, so you can see" (Revelation 3:17–18).

Jesus' kingdom is not a vision of an earthly Eden. Christ, who knows his way through the ruins of our lives, calls us to taste eternity now, on this earth and in this time. As we battle our wills, as we face temptations and pressures daily, we need to remember the words of the apostle Paul: "Who shall separate us from the love of Christ? Shall tribulation [tests and temptations], or distress [emotional pressures], or persecution [attacks from other kingdoms], or famine, or nakedness, or peril, or sword [all suffering]?" (Romans 8:35 RSV).

Paul knew that the King's character, not ours, would hold us through all circumstances. In response to God's love, we are called to treat others as though they bear the very image and likeness of God. This can happen only when our entire lives, including our temptations and struggles, are given to the King. Jesus taught us, as citizens of that future-yet-present kingdom, to say,

> Our Father who art in heaven,
> Hallowed be thy name.
> Thy kingdom come.
> Thy will be done in earth,
> as it is in heaven.
> Give us this day our daily bread.
> And forgive us our debts,
> as we forgive our debtors.
> And lead us not into temptation,
> but deliver us from evil.
> For thine is the kingdom,
> and the power, and the glory, for ever.
> Amen.

Notes

Chapter 1

1. James Stalker, *The World's Great Sermons* (London: Funk and Wagnalls), 171.
2. Jay E. Adams, *Competent to Counsel* (Philadelphia: Presbyterian and Reformed, 1970), 219.
3. Ibid., 211.
4. John White, *The Fight* (Downers Grove, Ill.: InterVarsity Press, 1976), 78.
5. Fulton Sheen, *Lift Up Your Hearts* (Garden City, N.Y.: Doubleday, 1955), 55.

Chapter 2

1. C. S. Lewis, *Mere Christianity* (New York: Macmillan, 1952).
2. Paul Tournier, *The Violence Within* (New York: Harper & Row, 1977), 44.
3. Lewis, *Mere Christianity*, 112.
4. Udo Middleman, *Pro-Existence* (Downers Grove, Ill.: InterVarsity Press, 1973), 99.

Chapter 3

1. John Knox, *The World's Great Sermons* (New York: Funk and Wagnalls, 1908), 178.
2. Henri Nouwen, "The Wilderness Temptations of Ministry," in *Leadership* (Fall 1982): 62.
3. John Calvin, *Commentary on Matthew* (Grand Rapids: Wm. B. Eerdmans, 1972), 135–37.
4. Fyodor Dostoevsky, *The Brothers Karamazov* (New York: Random House, 1955), 263.

Chapter 4

1. William Barclay, *The Gospel of Matthew.* Vol. 1. (Philadelphia: Westminster Press, 1965), 62.
2. Dostoevsky, *The Brothers Karamazov,* 265.
3. Barclay, *The Gospel of Matthew,* vol. 1, 62.
4. Nouwen, "The Wilderness Temptations of Ministry," 62–63.
5. John White, *Flirting With the World* (Wheaton, Ill.: Harold Shaw, 1982), 104–5.
6. Jacques Ellul, *The Presence of the Kingdom* (New York: Seabury, 1948), 79.
7. White, *Flirting With the World,* 109.
8. Dostoevsky, *The Brothers Karamazov,* 265.
9. Nouwen, "The Wilderness Temptations of Ministry," 62–63.

Chapter 5

1. Nouwen, "The Wilderness Temptations of Ministry," 63.
2. Anthony Campolo, *The Success Fantasy* (Wheaton, Ill.: Victor Books, 1980), 9.
3. Barbara Goldsmith, "The Meaning of Celebrity," in the *New York Times Magazine* (4 December 1983): 74.
4. Campolo, *The Success Fantasy,* 15.
5. Nouwen, "The Wilderness Temptations of Ministry," 63.

Chapter 6

1. David Augsburger, *Caring Enough to Forgive* (Ventura, Calif.: Regal Books, 1982), 12–13.
2. C. S. Lewis, *The Problem of Pain* (New York: Macmillan, 1960), 104.
3. George Eldon Ladd, *The Gospel of the Kingdom* (Grand Rapids: Wm. B. Eerdmans, 1959), 91.
4. Ray Stedman, *The Psalms* (Waco, Tex.: Word Books), 183.
5. Dan Hamilton, *Forgiveness* (Downers Grove, Ill.: InterVarsity Press, 1980), 13–14.
6. Fulton Sheen, *Walk With God* (New York: Maco Magazine Corp., 1965), 80.
7. Lewis, *The Problem of Pain,* 105–6.
8. Augsburger, *Caring Enough to Forgive.*
9. Hamilton, *Forgiveness,* 19, 23.
10. Ibid., 17.
11. John R. W. Stott, *Christian Counter-Culture* (Downers Grove, Ill.: InterVarsity Press, 1978), 149.
12. Adams, *Competent to Counsel,* 230.
13. Francis A. Schaeffer, *The Mark of the Christian* (Downers Grove, Ill.: InterVarsity Press, 1970), 16.

Chapter 7

1. Mario Jacoby, *On Anxiety and Guilt* (Zurich: Jung Institute Lectures, 1981), 46.
2. Ibid., 44.
3. Heinz L. Ansbacher and Rowena R. Ansbacher, *The Individual Psychology of Alfred Adler* (New York: Harper & Row, 1956), 256, 272–273.
4. Hal Lindsey, *Satan Is Alive and Well on Planet Earth* (New York: Bantam Books, 1974), 184.
5. Sheen, *Walk With God,* 46–47.
6. Earl Jabay, *Search for Identity* (Grand Rapids: Zondervan, 1967), 51.
7. White, *The Fight,* 83.
8. Fulton Sheen, *Peace of Soul* (Garden City, N.Y.: Doubleday, Image Books, 1949), 62–63.
9. White, *The Fight,* 84.
10. Ibid., 84.
11. Harold Busséll, *Unholy Devotion: Why Cults Lure Christians* (Grand Rapids: Zondervan, 1983), 75.
12. Dietrich Bonhoeffer, *Ethics* (New York: Macmillan, 1955), 111.
13. Lindsey, *Satan Is Alive and Well,* 198.
14. Ibid., 202.
15. David Johnson, *Reaching Out: Interpersonal Effectiveness and Self-Actualization* (Englewood Cliffs, N.J.: Prentice-Hall, 1972), 142–43.
16. Ibid., 144.

Chapter 8

1. Charles Durham, *Temptation* (Downers Grove, Ill.: InterVarsity Press, 1982), 32.
2. Peter Gillquist, "Spiritual Warfare: Bearing the Bruises of Battle," in *Christianity Today* (8 August 1980): 24–25.
3. Eric Fife, "The Benefits of Spiritual Failure," in *Eternity* (October 1971): 25–26.
4. Adams, *Competent to Counsel,* 141.
5. Vernon Grounds, "Faith for Failure" (Commencement Address, Gordon College, 21 May 1977).
6. Neil Clark Warren, "Self-Esteem: A Two-Track Approach," *Theology News and Notes* (December 1978): 3–4.
7. Paul Tournier, *The Adventure of Living* (New York: Harper & Row, 1963), 112-13.
8. Sheen, *Walk With God,* 56.
9. Stuart Briscoe, *What Works When Life Doesn't* (Wheaton, Ill.: Victor Books, 1977), 139.

Chapter 9

1. Durham, *Temptation*, 136.
2. Barclay, *The Gospel of Matthew*, vol. 1, 136.
3. Stott, *Christian Counter-Culture*, 150.
4. Anonymous, "The War Within: An Anatomy of Lust," in *Leadership* (Fall 1982): 46.
5. W. H. Lewis, ed., *Letters of C. S. Lewis* (New York: Harcourt Brace Jovanovich, 1966), 199.

Chapter 10

1. Thomas Howard, "The Last Lecture" (Convocation Address, Gordon College, 8 May 1982).

Chapter 11

1. John Calvin, *Institutes of the Christian Religion* (Grand Rapids: Wm. B. Eerdmans, 1972), vol. 1, book 1.
2. Jabay, *Search for Identity*, 80.
3. Ibid., 80–81.

Chapter 12

1. Ladd, *The Gospel of the Kingdom*, 19.
2. Ibid., 22.
3. John Bright, *The Kingdom of God* (Nashville: Pierce and Washabaugh, 1953), 223.

Bibliography

Books

Adams, Jay E. *Competent to Counsel.* Philadelphia: Presbyterian and Reformed Publishing Co., 1970.

Ansbacher, Heinz, and Rowena Ansbacher. *The Individual Psychology of Alfred Adler.*New York: Harper & Row, 1956.

Archer, Gleason L. *Encyclopedia of Bible Difficulties.* Grand Rapids: Zondervan, 1982.

Augsburger, David. *Caring Enough to Forgive.* Ventura, Calif.: Regal Books, 1982.

Barclay, William. *The Gospel of Matthew.* Vol. 1. Philadelphia: Westminster Press, 1965.

Bonhoeffer, Dietrich. *Ethics.* New York: Macmillan, 1955.

———. *Life Together.* New York: Harper & Row, 1954.

———. *Creation and Fall—Temptation.* New York: Macmillan, 1959.

Bright, John. *The Kingdom of God.* Nashville: Pierce and Washabaugh, 1953.

Briscoe, Stuart. *What Works When Life Doesn't.* Wheaton, Ill.: Victor Books, 1977.

Busséll, Harold. *Unholy Devotion: Why Cults Lure Christians.* Grand Rapids: Zondervan, 1983.

Calvin, John. *Institutes of the Christian Religion.* Grand Rapids: Wm. B. Eerdmans, 1972. 2 volumes.

———. *Commentary on Matthew.* Grand Rapids: Wm. B. Eerdmans, 1972.

Dostoevsky, Fyodor. *The Brothers Karamazov.* New York: Random House, 1955.

Durham, Charles. *Temptation.* Downers Grove, Ill.: InterVarsity Press, 1982.

Ellul, Jacques. *The Presence of the Kingdom.* New York: Seabury Press, 1948. 2nd ed. 1967.

Griffiths, Michael. *Unsplitting Your Christian Life.* Downers Grove, Ill.: InterVarsity Press, 1960.

Haile, Peter. *The Difference God Makes.* Downers Grove, Ill.: InterVarsity Press, 1981.

Heschel, Abraham. *God in Search of Man: A Philosophy of Judaism.* New York: Farrar, Straus and Giroux, 1976.

______. *The Insecurity of Freedom.* New York: Schocken Books, 1972.

Jabay, Earl. *Search for Identity.* Grand Rapids: Zondervan, 1967.

Jacoby, Mario. *On Anxiety and Guilt.* Zurich: Jung Institute Lectures, 1981.

Jaspers, Karl. *The Way to Wisdom.* New Haven: Yale University Press, 1951.

Johnson, David. *Reaching Out.* Englewood Cliffs, N.J.: Prentice-Hall, 1972.

Jones, E. Stanley. *Is the Kingdom of God Realism?* New York: Abingdon Cokesbury Press.

Knox, John. *The World's Great Sermons.* New York: Funk and Wagnalls, 1908.

Kuyper, Abraham. *The Work of the Holy Spirit.* Grand Rapids: Wm. B. Eerdmans, 1979.

Ladd, George Eldon. *The Gospel of the Kingdom.* Grand Rapids: Wm. B. Eerdmans, 1959.

Lewis, C. S. *Mere Christianity.* New York: Macmillan, 1952.

Lewis, W. H., ed. *Letters of C. S. Lewis.* New York: Harcourt Brace Jovanovich, 1966.

Lindsey, Hal. *Satan Is Alive and Well on Planet Earth.* New York: Bantam Books, 1974.

Massey, John. *Great Ideas.* A collection of quotes printed by the Container Corporation of America, 1976.

McDonald, Gordon. *Facing Turbulent Times.* Wheaton, Ill.: Tyndale House, 1981.

Middleman, Udo. *Pro-Existence.* Downers Grove, Ill.: InterVarsity Press, 1973.

Muggeridge, Malcolm. *Jesus the Man Who Lives.* New York: Harper & Row, 1975.

Niebuhr, H. Richard. *Radical Monotheism and Western Culture.* London: Faber and Faber, 1960.

———. *Christ and Culture.* New York: Harper & Row, 1951.

Packer, J. I. *Knowing God.* Downers Grove, Ill.: InterVarsity Press, 1973.

Palmer, Earl. *The Intimate Gospel.* Waco, Tex.: Word Books, 1978.

Parker, Larry. *We Let Our Son Die.* Irvine, Calif.: Harvest House, 1980.

Peterson, Eugene H. *A Long Obedience in the Same Direction.* Downers Grove, Ill.: InterVarsity Press, 1980.

Ridderbos, Herman. *The Coming of the Kingdom.* Philadelphia: Presbyterian and Reformed, 1962.

Schaeffer, Edith. *Lifelines.* Westchester, Ill.: Crossway Books, 1982.

Schaeffer, Frankie. *Addicted to Mediocrity.* Westchester, Ill.: Cornerstone, 1981.

Seerveld, Calvin. *Rainbows for the Fallen World.* Toronto: Tuppence Press, 1980.

Sheen, Fulton. *Lift Up Your Hearts.* Garden City, N.Y.: Doubleday, 1955.

———. *Peace of Soul.* Garden City, N.Y.: Doubleday, 1949.

———. *Walk With God.* New York: Maco Magazine Corp., 1965.

Stalker, James. *The World's Great Sermons.* London: Funk and Wagnalls.

Stott, John R. W. *Christian Counter-Culture.* Downers Grove, Ill.: InterVarsity Press, 1978.

Tournier, Paul. *The Adventure of Living.* New York: Harper & Row, 1963.

———. *The Violence Within.* New York: Harper & Row, 1977.

White, John. *The Fight.* Downers Grove, Ill.: InterVarsity Press, 1976.

———. *Flirting With the World.* Wheaton, Ill.: Harold Shaw, 1982.

Lectures

Grounds, Vernon. "Faith for Failure." Commencement address given at Gordon College, 21 May 1977.

Howard, Thomas O. *The Last Lecture.* Convocation address given at Gordon College, 8 May 1982.

Periodicals

Busséll, Harold. "When Your Child Goes Astray." *Family Life* (May 1982).

Chapman, J. Wilber. *Insights* (Summer 1981).

Gillquist, Peter. "Spiritual Warfare: Bearing the Bruises of Battle." *Christianity Today* (8 August 1980).

Nouwen, Henri. "The Wilderness Temptations of Ministry." *Leadership* 3, no. 4 (Fall 1982).

Warren, Neil Clark. "Self-Esteem." *Theology News and Notes* (December 1978).

Anonymous. "The War Within: An Anatomy of Lust." *Leadership* 3, no. 4 (Fall 1982).

Recordings

Atlanta Rhythm Section. "Imaginary Lovers." *Champagne Jam.* Polydor Inc., 1978.